AMPHITRYON 38

Plays by S. N. Behrman

Amphitryon 38

A COMEDY IN A PROLOGUE AND

THREE ACTS BY Jean Giraudoux

ADAPTED FROM THE FRENCH BY

S. N. Behrman

RANDOM HOUSE · NEW YORK

MANUFACTURED IN THE UNITED STATES OF AMERICA

For

JEAN GIRAUDOUX

With the hope that the American version
of his enchanting play will afford him,
occasionally, some gleam of recognition.

AMPHITRYON 38 was produced by the Theatre Guild, Inc., at the Schubert Theatre on November 2, 1937, with the following cast:

(in the order in which they speak)

JUPITER	Alfred Lunt
MERCURY	Richard Whorf
SOSIE, SERVANT TO AMPHITRYON	George Meader
TRUMPETER	Sydney Greenstreet
WARRIOR	Alan Hewitt
ALKMENA	Lynn Fontanne
AMPHITRYON	Barry Thomson
NEVETZA	Kathleen Roland
KLEANTHA	Jacqueline Paige
ECHO	Ernestine De Becker
LEDA	Edith King

The action takes place in and about Amphitryon's palace

Directed by Bretaigne Windust
Settings by Lee Simonson
Costumes by Valentina
Music composed by Samuel L. M. Barlow

PROLOGUE

PROLOGUE

Scene: *A Cloud*.

JUPITER, *the master of the gods, and* MERCURY, *his half-son,
are lounging on a cloud, their phosphorescent eyes focused for
the moment on the domesticities of a terrestrial couple.*

JUPITER

(*Peering straight out*)

There she is, Mercury—there she is!

MERCURY

Where, Jupiter, where?

JUPITER

You see that lighted window, the one with the curtain stirring in the breeze? She's there. Alkmena is there! No, now
she's gone! Don't move, don't move—in a second perhaps, you
will see her shadow pass again.

MERCURY

Jupiter, you astonish me. If you're in love with this mortal,
why don't you employ the facilities you have as a god? Why
waste an entire night, ravished with longing, bouncing about

on a cloud, catching at her shadow when you might so easily, with your ordinary god-sight, see her as she is through the walls of her chamber.

JUPITER

You would have me caress her body with invisible hands, enfold her in a closeness she could not feel?

MERCURY

But the wind makes love like that, Jupiter, and the wind is as much as you are, one of the prime elements of fecundity.

JUPITER

True, but with her, Mercury, I am tempted to transcend my former conquests. I have a nostalgia for mortality. I would like to experience the same difficulties human beings do—and the same delights. As a god, I feel I should be closer to my subjects!

MERCURY

Oh, but love-making among human beings is such a boring routine!

JUPITER

Oh, you think so, do you?

MERCURY

Yes. To begin with, you must woo her—then you must undress her—then you must dress her again. And to get rid of her you must actively antagonize her,—it's a full time job!

JUPITER

Yes, it's true that the rituals and conventions of earthly love-making are complicated—but strangely enough, it is their strict observance that yields the greater pleasure.

MERCURY

I know them all. First you must follow her—

JUPITER

Measuring your pace exactly to hers so that both your legs seem to swing from the same fulcrum—

MERCURY

(*Rather bored, succumbing to the rhythm of a well-worn formula*)

Identifying in both your bodies the ultimate source of all impulse and all rhythm.

JUPITER

Then—with a bound, you are at her side—

MERCURY

With your left hand you descend on her breasts—

JUPITER

With your right hand you cover her eyelids—the most sensitive part of a woman's skin—

13

MERCURY

So that she may divine from the heat of your palm, your ardor—

JUPITER

And from the lines of your palm, your ultimate destiny, your mortal future and your grievous death. So that pity will stir in her as well as desire—

JUPITER and MERCURY
(*Together*)

For in the conquest of a woman—the one is as important as the other—

JUPITER

Acquiescent at last—you undo her girdle—

MERCURY and JUPITER
(*Together—in choir*)

And so forth—and so forth—and so forth—

JUPITER

And then what do you do?

MERCURY

And then what do I do?

JUPITER

Yes. What do you feel?

14

MERCURY

What do I feel? Nothing! Nothing special. In fact it's exactly like being with Venus!

JUPITER

Why then do you bother to go to Earth at all?

MERCURY

Out of boredom. And I confess that for a brief sojourn the Earth has certain advantages. What with its moist atmosphere and its green lawns it is perhaps the pleasantest planet on which to alight—but only for a brief stay—because it has distinct drawbacks. Due to its heavy mineral and oil deposits, it gives off a heady odor. It is, in fact, the only star which smells exactly like a wild animal.

JUPITER

Look at that curtain—look quickly!

MERCURY

Her shadow—

JUPITER

No, no. Not yet her shadow. What you see now is but the shadow of her shadow.

MERCURY

(Peering intently)

Well, whatever it is—that silhouette is dividing itself like a draw-bridge. There are two people there—interlaced like a

15

vine-motif in a frieze. It's not your unborn son, Jupiter, that makes that shadow so grossly convex but simply—her husband. (*In amazement*) Why, he's a giant! Look; he approaches her again—he embraces her again—he's insatiable!

JUPITER

Yes. Amphitryon, her only love.

MERCURY

Now, I begin to see why you are willing to forego your celestial eyesight. To observe merely a shadow-husband embracing a shadow wife is less painful than to observe the living substance. (*Short pause*) Now the shadow has disappeared!

JUPITER

Doubtless, overcome, she has sunk down and abandons herself to blissful languor—drinking in the songs of the ravished nightingales. Oh, happy, happy nightingales!

MERCURY

Ravished nightingales! Jupiter, you know perfectly well that as far as women are concerned these little birds are quite disinterested. In love affairs the nightingales are nothing but obligato. It's for that reason you have never found it advantageous to impersonate a nightingale. On several occasions you've had to do a bull—but never a nightingale! No, it's not the birds you have to worry about—it's the husband—the husband of this dark, lusty beauty!

16

JUPITER

(*Quickly*)

How do you know she's dark? Are you inventing, or are you spying?

MERCURY

I confess a moment ago, while she was in her bath, I resumed for a fleeting instant my celestial vision. Don't be annoyed—now I see no more than you do.

JUPITER

You're lying! I can tell it from your face. You're looking at her. You see her. I can see a glow on your face that comes only from the phosphorescence of a woman.

MERCURY

I confess—I am looking at her.

JUPITER

Well, what's she doing?

MERCURY

She is leaning over the relaxed Amphitryon. She's laughing. She holds Amphitryon's head in her hands as if she were weighing it. She kisses his head—she lets it fall back as if her kisses made it too heavy to hold. Now she is facing us squarely— Yes—she is indubitably—dark!

JUPITER

And her husband?

MERCURY

Quite dark. His nipples apricot—

JUPITER

I'm not interested in his color scheme. What is he doing?

MERCURY

He polishes her with his hand as one would a favorite pony. He's a celebrated horseman, you know.

JUPITER

And Alkmena?

MERCURY

Oh, so gay—so docile—so faithful.

JUPITER

Faithful to herself or faithful to her husband—that is the question. You know, Mercury, most faithful wives are unfaithful to their husbands with everything except men; with jewels—with perfumes—with reading—with religion and with the contemplation of Spring, with everything in fact, except a man. Don't you think these faithful wives deserve some compensation?

MERCURY

But Alkmena is faithful only to her husband! Jupiter, by what subterfuge can you make her yours?

18

JUPITER

The difficulty with these virtuous wives is not to seduce them—but to persuade them that they may be seduced confidentially! And the contemplation of this creature paralyzes my invention. What do you suggest, Mercury?

MERCURY

Functioning as a human being or functioning as a god?

JUPITER

How would the methods differ?

MERCURY

Well, functioning as a god—very simple. You lift her to our plane—you make her comfortable on a cloud—for the required seconds you let her bear a hero's weight—and then— you let her resume her own.

JUPITER

But by following that course I should forego the most exquisite sensation to be had from the love of a woman.

MERCURY

Which most exquisite sensation? There are several.

JUPITER

The moment of consent. But with Alkmena that's impossible because she loves only her husband.

MERCURY

Well, then—be her husband!

JUPITER

But he's never out of her sight! The most persistent stay-at-homes in the world are heroes out-of-work! They're more domestic than tigers!

MERCURY

Then employ him. Fortunately there is an infallible recipe for getting heroes out of the house.

JUPITER

War?

MERCURY

Have Thebes declare war.

JUPITER

But Thebes is at peace with her enemies.

MERCURY

Then have her declare war against a friend. What are friendly powers for if they can't have a little squabble now and then?

JUPITER

Isn't it singular, Mercury, you and I are gods and yet to achieve human simplicity becomes for us the most devious

20

exercise in style. While we are on Earth fate demands far more of us than she does of mortals. To obtain from Alkmena this exquisite consent—which the most grotesque of human beings can gain by making a few faces—we have to contrive innumerable stratagems, perform wonders, pile up miracles—

MERCURY

Well, contrive them! Pile them up!

JUPITER

How? How?

MERCURY

Have a warrior overcome by an uncontrollable impulse to exercise his profession. Instantly Amphitryon will fly off to head his army.

JUPITER

Of course!

MERCURY

The minute he is gone—assume his appearance—assign to me the exterior of his servant Sosie. I will appear—whisper discreetly in Alkmena's ear that Amphitryon has only made a pretense of departing—that actually he means to return—to spend the night with her.

JUPITER
(*With admiration*)
Oh, Mercury, you are your father's son!

21

MERCURY

Let us go—let us descend. Order a special cloud, Jupiter, to conceal us.

JUPITER

That's hardly necessary, Mercury. For there, on Earth, they have an institution which renders them invisible to creditors, to the jealous—which gives them surcease from their little nervous cares—a great and democratic institution—the only one—I may add—which is even moderately successful—

MERCURY

What is that, Jupiter?

JUPITER

The night!
(*The curtains close in and the lights fade as the music swells.*)

MERCURY

The night?

JUPITER

The night . . .

MERCURY

The night.

Curtain

ACT ONE

ACT ONE

Scene: *The façade and terrace of* AMPHITRYON's *palace in Thebes. Four rectangular steps. At top of fourth step is an iron grille gate. More steps from gate up to portico of Palace. The gate is open.*

Time: *Night.*

The TRUMPETER *is discovered with his trumpet.* SOSIE *enters from palace with scroll.*

SOSIE

Are you the Trumpeter of the day?

TRUMPETER

If I may make so bold, yes. And you, who are you, may I ask? You look like someone I know.

SOSIE
(*Importantly*)

I doubt it very much. I am Sosie. I am the servant, Official Announcer and Scribe to General Amphitryon. I am unique.

TRUMPETER
(*Humbly*)

I must be mistaken.

SOSIE

What are you waiting for? If you are the Trumpeter of the day, why don't you trumpet?

TRUMPETER

But, may I make so bold, your announcement? What does it announce?

SOSIE

You'll find out.

TRUMPETER

Is it Lost and Found? Has someone lost something?

SOSIE

On the contrary! Something has been found. Blow, I tell you.

TRUMPETER

(*Sits comfortably on top step*)

It's easy to say blow but how can I blow when I don't know what it is I'm blowing for?

SOSIE

You have no choice. You always blow the same note anyway.

TRUMPETER

(*With dignity*)

It is true my instrument has only one note but as for me personally I have many. For I am a composer. I compose hymns.

26

SOSIE

I bet your hymns have only one note. Hurry up, there's a good fellow, and blow. There's Orion in the sky already!

TRUMPETER
(*Placidly*)

Orion may be in the sky but that does not alter the fact that as a creative artist I have to know what it is you expect me to blow about. If I have attained any celebrity among the one-note trumpeters it is because, before blowing, I compose in my mind a whole musical composition of which the last note is invariably the one I blow. That note is the climax. That is why, when I do come to blow it, it has such surprise, such brilliance, such finality. The climax may be always the same but the approach—ah!—the approach . . . !

SOSIE

I wish for once you'd begin with the climax! The whole town's falling asleep!

TRUMPETER

The town may be falling asleep, but I must just stop to tell you that my colleagues, in fact all trumpeters, are consumed with jealousy of me. You can see why—because none of them are composers. They tell me that in the trumpet-schools they have instituted, thanks to my example, a course, teaching the trumpeters not to blow, indeed, but how to perfect the silence that precedes the blowing. Now you can see, I am sure, how important it is for me to know what it is I'm blowing for.

27

First, I have to compose a silent air and how can I do that if I don't know whether I'm blowing for war or for peace, for Lost and Found or for marriage, or birth or death. I've got to know, that's all!

SOSIE

Well then it's for peace.

TRUMPETER

What peace?

SOSIE

At least what passes for peace—the breathing-spell between wars.

TRUMPETER

Shall I compose something martial?

SOSIE

For peace!

TRUMPETER

It has been my observation that a martial air is irresistible no matter what the cause. I myself, pacific nature though I am, when I hear a military-band, feel truculent. I can't help it. Shall I do something of the sort for peace?

SOSIE

If it's not misleading . . . ?

28

TRUMPETER

Leave it to me! (*The* TRUMPETER *lifts his instrument to his lips, weaving meanwhile with his free hand a stirring, military air.* SOSIE *interrupts impatiently.*)

SOSIE

Don't be too warlike!

TRUMPETER

(*Patiently regretful*)

Now I have to begin all over again. . . . (*He repeats the business and blows his one note. Magnanimously*) Now you may deliver. . . .

SOSIE

(*Declaiming*)

The General Amphitryon has bade me address you on the subject of Peace. . . . I don't see a single light down there. I'm afraid your wonderful trumpet didn't carry far!

TRUMPETER

Ah! But they heard my silent song—it entered their ears insensibly—that is all I ask.

SOSIE

(*Continuing his proclamation*)

Oh, Thebans! The General Amphitryon, whose war proclamations have so often stirred you, has asked me to deliver you a peace proclamation. Instead of rousing you from your beds it is intended to lull you to a deeper sleep. Is it not good to

29

sleep in a fatherland unscarred by the trenches of war, among friendly birds and dogs and cats, among rats whose appetites have never been whetted by the taste of human flesh? Is it not good to wear your national countenance, not as a mask to frighten those who haven't the same blood-count you have but as an oval mirror to reflect smiling and laughter? Thebans, sleep!

TRUMPETER

That's good! That's very good! Did General Amphitryon write that?

SOSIE

General Amphitryon is too busy to write! I am his scribe. I wrote it.

TRUMPETER

Did he give you the ideas?

SOSIE

He simply said: Deliver them a Peace Proclamation. They're my own ideas!

TRUMPETER

Nevertheless, they're good! They're very good!

SOSIE

(*Continuing*)

Thebans! You may sleep! What more lovely array than your unarmed and naked bodies, flat on your backs, arms outstretched with nothing heavier to worry about than your navels. . . . Never has there been a night so transfigured, so fragrant, so serene . . . sleep! sleep! sleep!

TRUMPETER
(*Made sleepy by the cadence*)
I'd like to take a nap myself. . . .

SOSIE
Now, then, Thebans! (*He pulls out a scroll and reads from it*) The General Amphitryon has ordered me to read you, instead of a War Bulletin—a Peace Bulletin. Listen: Between the Issus and its tributary we have taken an important prisoner, a roebuck wandered from Thrace. Around Mount Olympus, by dint of skillful maneuvering, we have coaxed the arid plains into a fine green sward which presently will blossom into wheat! The syringas we have caused to be lanced by great swarms of bees. On the shores of the Aegean there is nothing, neither in the expanse of the waves nor in the vista of the stars to burden the spirit with apprehension and, in the mysterious distances that separate the temples from the firmament, the trees from the houses, animals from men, we have ambushed a thousand secret signals which our wise men will be centuries in deciphering . . . we are menaced, Thebans, by centuries of peace. . . . Cursed be war! Cursed be war! Cursed be war! (*The* WARRIOR *enters.*)

TRUMPETER
(*Murmuring sympathetically out of his drowse*)
Cursed be war . . . !

WARRIOR
(*Fiercely*)

What is that you say?

SOSIE
(*Frightened*)

I repeat what I have just said: "A curse on war!"

WARRIOR

Do you know to whom you are saying this?

SOSIE

I do not.

WARRIOR

To a professional warrior.

TRUMPETER
(*Fully awake now*)

Ah! Now we'll get a different point of view!

SOSIE

Well, there are wars and wars!

WARRIOR

Not to a warrior. Where is your master?

SOSIE

There—in his bedroom—where the light is burning.

32

WARRIOR

Bring your master this message instantly. He must get into his accoutrements at once.

SOSIE

He's asleep.

WARRIOR

Take him the message at once! It's war!

SOSIE

But from everywhere resounds that murmur which old men call the echo of peace!

WARRIOR

And that, my friend, is just the moment for me!

SOSIE

War! Again!

TRUMPETER

What do you mean again? Still!

WARRIOR

The Athenians have mobilized their troops and crossed the frontier.

SOSIE

You lie! The Athenians are our allies!

WARRIOR

Then it is our allies who are invading us—wake up Amphityon. Do you hear? Go! (SOSIE *exits into the palace.*)

33

WARRIOR

(*To the* TRUMPETER *who starts to follow* SOSIE)
You stay here! Blow your trumpet!

TRUMPETER

What is the subject on which you wish me to blow?

WARRIOR

War!

TRUMPETER

But which aspect of war? Do you wish me to emphasize its
sublime side or its pathetic side?

WARRIOR

Neither. I want you to emphasize its appeal to Youth. (*The*
TRUMPETER *composes and blows. The* WARRIOR *leans over the*
balustrade and shouts) Thebans awake! All of you who are
vital, whose bodies are strong and unblemished, segregate
yourselves from the sweating mass spawning there in the
darkness. Get up! To arms!

TRUMPETER

Some of those lazy people would rather spawn! They're
very weak.

WARRIOR

(*Continues his harangue*)
You who are poor, all of you whom fortune has treated
badly, war will restore your rights. And you rich come and

xperience the final ecstasy—the ecstasy of the gambler who
isks his position, his pleasures, his mistresses, on one turn of
he wheel. You zealots, you prayerful ones, make Nationalism
our religion. And you atheists and sensualists, war is your
paradise for it legalizes all your excesses—you may whet your
words on the statues of the gods themselves. You who hate
work—to the trenches—war is the heaven of the lazy. And
or you who are industrious—we have the Commissariat!

TRUMPETER

There's something in what he says—jobs for everybody!

WARRIOR

Get up! Fall into rank! For who prefers to the glory of
dying valiantly for one's country the inglorious destiny of stay-
ng at home overfed, lethargic and slothful?

TRUMPETER

I do.

WARRIOR

Besides, Citizens, there is nothing really to be afraid of. I
nay tell you this in confidence: in this war, on our side at
east, there will be no fatalities whatever, and moreover, what-
ver wounds there are will be in the left hand—except among
he left-handed. No more petty squabbles—war unites us! And
ow humane it is, for it abolishes the barbaric duel! Here she
s—your war, ready for you, eager to welcome you. War!
Welcome! I salute you! War! It's begun already. See the

35

lights down there. Citizens—to arms! (*He comes down the steps hurriedly shouting as he goes*) You may pick your laws, your pleasures, your women—Liberty, Equality, Fraternity, War— (*He rushes across the stage shouting slogans*) Freedom—license—cruelty—joy—war— (*His voice trails off as he disappears.* SOSIE *enters from the palace.*)

TRUMPETER

(*To* SOSIE)

Your master is ready?

SOSIE

He is ready. It is my mistress who isn't quite ready. It takes no time at all to dress for going to war, but to dress for saying farewell takes longer.

TRUMPETER

Is she one of those weeping women?

SOSIE

Unfortunately one of the smiling ones. The weeping ones regain their composure more quickly than the smiling ones.

TRUMPETER

(*Shrugs his shoulders philosophically, then looks down on the city below*)

They're getting up all right. Look at those lights! (*He rises and starts coming down the steps*) He'll get 'em. (*He crosses the stage ruminating out loud*) They could sleep in peace but

hey'd rather get up and fight. . . . They like it. They want it.
Well, if that's what they want they can have it. (*He goes out
dejectedly.* SOSIE *comes down the steps and follows him.*)

SOSIE

What miserable luck—to have this happen on the very day
hat Peace is proclaimed! (*He goes out.* AMPHITRYON *enters
from palace, in full war regalia. He goes to end of platform,
cans the horizon and starts down steps.* ALKMENA *enters from
he palace.*)

ALKMENA

Amphitryon! I love you— (AMPHITRYON *quickly goes up
teps, embraces her and kisses her.*)

AMPHITRYON

I love you, Alkmena.

ALKMENA

Will you think of me while you're away? Do you promise
t?

AMPHITRYON

Yes, darling. (*Looks away.*)

ALKMENA

Why do you turn to the moon? I'm jealous of the moon—
hat blank surface—what thoughts do you get from her?

37

AMPHITRYON

And from your dark head—what?

ALKMENA

A scent at least—twin brother of memory. Oh, you'r
shaved! Do they shave now to go to war? Do you think witl
your skin pumiced like that, you'll be more formidable?

AMPHITRYON

Oh, no, darling. For that I rely on my armor and helmet.

ALKMENA

Put your helmet on. Let me see you as your enemy sees you

AMPHITRYON

Now don't be frightened! (*Puts helmet on.*)

ALKMENA

Not very frightening—not when those eyes are your eyes.

AMPHITRYON

But to my enemy it is, I assure you.

ALKMENA

What are your greaves made of?

AMPHITRYON

Silver—chased in platinum.

38

ALKMENA

Aren't they too tight for you? Wouldn't steel ones be more flexible for running?

AMPHITRYON

My dear, I'm a general in command—and generals in command never run. (*Horses' hoofs heard off stage.*)

ALKMENA

Your horses, your horses are here. Kiss me.

AMPHITRYON

No, no, my horses have quite a different gait—but that's no reason why I can't kiss you. (*They kiss.*)

ALKMENA

Is your helmet silver, too?

AMPHITRYON

The purest.

ALKMENA

What color tunic are you wearing beneath your armor?

AMPHITRYON

Rose-pink—edged with black braid.

ALKMENA

Oh, you naughty Amphitryon! How coquettish you are with your war!—Rose-pink—black braid. Does that help you to achieve your victories, or do you win them in one head-long charge, my name on your lips?

AMPHITRYON

No, darling, it isn't that way.

ALKMENA

How do you do it then?

AMPHITRYON

Well, first of all I surround their left wing with my right wing, then I divide their right wing—using only three-quarters of my left wing—and then with the remaining quarter of my left wing I dart in among them—

ALKMENA

I see. A kind of battle of the birds.

AMPHITRYON

—and that gives me the victory.

ALKMENA

How many victories have you won, dearest one?

AMPHITRYON

One, just one.

ALKMENA

Well, tell me, Amphitryon, have you killed many men?

AMPHITRYON

One, only one.

ALKMENA

How economical you are, dear. Was he a king? Was he a
general?

AMPHITRYON

No, he was a simple soldier.

ALKMENA

So modest—modest to a fault, my dear. Tell me, did you,
in the process of his destruction, did you allow him one instant in which to recognize you and be aware of the distinction you had just conferred on him? Did you, sweetheart?

AMPHITRYON

Yes, I did. Blood pouring out of his mouth, he looked up at
me and managed, with his last breath, a faint, respectful smile.

ALKMENA

He must have been very happy! Did he tell you his name
before he died?

AMPHITRYON

He was an anonymous soldier—there are quite a few of
them.

ALKMENA

I see! You know, darling, when you breathe your armor
loosens at the fastenings, and your tunic gives your skin a tint

of dawn. Breathe, Amphitryon, breathe—deeply—and let me savor, in the darkness of this night, the glow of your body. Stay a little longer. (*Presses closely to him*) Do you love me?

AMPHITRYON

Yes. I have to wait for my horses anyway. Darling, don't press too closely to me—you'll hurt yourself. You know I'm a husband made of iron.

ALKMENA

Can you feel me—through all that armor?

AMPHITRYON

Through every chink where an arrow might reach me, you reach me. And you—do you feel me?

ALKMENA

Yes—but your own body is a kind of armor. Often I have lain in your arms and felt you remoter and colder than I do now.

AMPHITRYON

Alkmena, often I have held you close to me, and felt you sadder and more desolate than I feel you today. And yet, on those occasions I was departing not for the war but for the hunt. (ALKMENA *smiles*) Now, why do you smile? Do you find consolation in this sudden declaration of war?

42

ALKMENA

Did you hear a child crying beneath our window a little while ago? Didn't that seem to you to be a premonition of evil?

AMPHITRYON

No, no, no. Omens are always announced with a thunder-clap in a clear sky, accompanied by a triple flash of lightning.

ALKMENA

The sky was clear and yet the child was crying. That seemed to me to be even a worse augury.

AMPHITRYON

Don't be superstitious, Alkmena.

ALKMENA

Something was hovering over our happiness. Praise be to the gods it was only war.

AMPHITRYON

Why do you say that—only war?

ALKMENA

I was afraid it was our love that might be threatened—it's there I feel the danger. I almost find consolation in war. At least, it's a tangible and visible antagonist. I like enemies whose weapons I can see—my great fear has always been that I would one day find you in the arms of other women.

43

AMPHITRYON

Other women!

ALKMENA

One or a thousand—what difference does it make? You'd
be lost.

AMPHITRYON

You are the most beautiful woman in all Thebes.

ALKMENA

It's the goddesses I'm afraid of—and those foreigners.

AMPHITRYON

You're not serious.

ALKMENA

Above all—I fear the goddesses. When they emerge from
the heavens—rosy without rouge—pearly without powder—
their breasts whiter than snow and their arms stronger than
crowbars, it must be very difficult to resist them. Don't you
think so?

AMPHITRYON

For anyone but me it might be—yes.

ALKMENA

But they're very sensitive, they take offense at very little,
and they like to be loved. You've never loved a goddess, have
you?

44

AMPHITRYON

Certainly not.

ALKMENA

No goddess has ever loved you?

AMPHITRYON

No.

ALKMENA

Not a little tiny bit?

AMPHITRYON

No! And what's more, I never loved a foreigner, either.

ALKMENA

They've loved you.

AMPHITRYON

Oh, no, they haven't.

ALKMENA

Oh, yes, they have.

AMPHITRYON

Oh, but they have not, dear.

ALKMENA

Oh, they love every married man, these women. When they arrive in our cities everything is over for us, the stay-at-homes.

Even the ugly ones, they flaunt their ugliness because after all it's a foreign ugliness and therefore very provocative. They are in love with themselves because even to themselves they are foreign. Compared to a threat like that war comes as a friend. You won't be killed, will you? Generals in command are never killed. You will come back.

AMPHITRYON

I'll be back very soon, and that will be forever. (*They kiss.*)

ALKMENA

Look! The stars are twinkling harder than ever. It is their last chance before dawn and our parting. Which one of them shall we choose to fix our eyes on tomorrow and every night at this same hour?

AMPHITRYON

Well, there's always our old friend Venus!

ALKMENA

I don't trust her. As an intermediary in love she might turn out to be not quite so disinterested. No, that side of my life I'd rather look after personally.

AMPHITRYON

What about Jupiter? There's a good solid name!

ALKMENA

I'd rather have a star that has no name.

46

AMPHITRYON

What about that little one over there that's called anonymous star.

ALKMENA

Well, that's a name, isn't it? (*Horses' hoofs heard.*)

AMPHITRYON

This time it's they—I must go. (*Starts down steps.*)

ALKMENA

Who are "they"? Your ambition, your pride as a commander, your love for carnage and adventure?

AMPHITRYON

No, no. Just Elaphocephale and Hypsipila, my horses.

ALKMENA

(*Comes down steps*)

Go then if you must.

AMPHITRYON

Is that all you have to say to me?

ALKMENA

Haven't I said about everything? What do other wives say?

AMPHITRYON

Well—they make jokes. They hand you your shield and they say things like "Return on it or beneath it!" They cry

47

out after you, "Fear nothing," "Do or die!" Can it be that my wife has no gift for epigrams like that?

ALKMENA

I'm afraid not. I couldn't utter a phrase that belonged more to posterity than it did to you. The only words that I can find to utter are those which perish softly even as they touch you. I love you, Amphitryon! Come back soon, Amphitryon! Besides, your name is so long, once you've said it there's hardly breath left to follow it up with an immortal sentence. (SOSIE *enters with* AMPHITRYON'S *spear and shield*.)

AMPHITRYON

Then say my name at the end. (*Takes spear and shield from* SOSIE *and lifts his right arm in a salute*) Good-bye, Alkmena! (*Exits, followed by* SOSIE.)

ALKMENA

Amphitryon! (*For a moment she stands still. Then the sound of horses' hoofs is heard starting and then gradually diminishing in the distance.* ALKMENA, *on the verge of sobbing, turns away.* MERCURY, *disguised as* SOSIE, *enters and stands below gate.* ALKMENA *turns to gate, looks at* MERCURY *in amazement, knowing that* SOSIE *had just gone off, laughs nervously and looks at him again.* MERCURY *gives her the keys to the gate; she closes gate but does not lock it and starts up steps.*)

ALKMENA
(*As she starts up steps*)

Good night, Sosie.

MERCURY

Alkmena, my lady Alkmena—

ALKMENA

What is it, Sosie?

MERCURY

I have a message for you from my master.

ALKMENA

From your master? Your master is still within earshot.

MERCURY

Exactly, my lady. No one must hear. My master has instructed me to inform you that he is only pretending to leave with the army, that actually he means to return to spend this night with you, once he's given his orders. . . .

ALKMENA

I don't understand you, Sosie. (*Goes up another step.*)

MERCURY

(*Repeating mechanically*)

My master has instructed me to inform you that—

ALKMENA

How dull you are, Sosie! Don't you understand the first principle of keeping a secret—which is to pretend the moment you've heard it—the moment you've grasped it—not to know a thing about it?

49

MERCURY

Very good, my lady. . . .

ALKMENA

As a matter of fact I haven't understood one word you've been saying.

MERCURY

You must sit up and watch for my master, my lady. . . .

ALKMENA

Yes, yes, Sosie. Stop chattering. (*Goes up the rest of the steps*) Isn't the wind blowing your tongue about? (*Exits into palace.* MERCURY *looks up at the sky above him and guardedly whispers hoarsely.*)

MERCURY

Jupiter! Jupiter! (*Motions with his thumb that* ALKMENA *is inside waiting. There is a terrific crash offstage.* MERCURY *rushes off.* JUPITER *enters dressed exactly as* AMPHITRYON, *carrying shield and spear.* MERCURY *follows* JUPITER.)

MERCURY

Are you all right?

JUPITER

Yes. I forgot the law of gravity. (JUPITER *boldly starts toward gate.*)

50

MERCURY

Where are you going?

JUPITER

I'm going in!

MERCURY

You can't do that.

JUPITER

Why not? I've copied his costume down to the last detail.

MERCURY

There's an element here that goes beyond costume. Look at you! You've just emerged from the brambles and there isn't a scratch on you! And no creases! Even clothes from the best tailors have creases the moment you've worn them. Turn around. (*Takes shield and spear from* JUPITER *and puts them down.*)

JUPITER

What?

MERCURY

Turn around!

JUPITER

Gods never turn around.

MERCURY

But I must see your back!

JUPITER

Why?

MERCURY

Men think that women never notice their backs. They are unaware that although they pretend to be overcome by their magnificent padded chests, they are actually maliciously scrutinizing the back view. It's from the back that women estimate a man. (JUPITER *turns his back to him*) That's better. Your entire body must be faultless. Come here, so I can adjust your human uniform, also. (JUPITER *takes off his helmet and gives it to* MERCURY.)

JUPITER

Mercury, aren't my eyes good?

MERCURY

No, they're far too brilliant . . . all iris and no tear duct. You may have to cry, you know. (JUPITER *begins to cry.* MERCURY *snaps fingers*) There, there. (*Straightens* JUPITER *up*) Tell me, on your other adventures didn't you use pupils?

JUPITER

Pupils? I don't remember. Oh, you mean pupils—like this? (*Looks at* MERCURY *in a strange manner.*)

MERCURY

(*Cowering*)

No phosphorescence! No cat's eyes, please! (JUPITER *assumes his natural look*) There, that's better. Now, about your skin. (*Puts helmet down next to shield and spear.*)

JUPITER

What's wrong with my skin? (*Looking at his hands.*)

MERCURY

It's a baby's skin. To begin with we must have a weather-beaten skin—a skin on which the wind has blown for thirty years. In short, a well-seasoned skin—a skin that may be tasted. For tasted it will be. Didn't they complain, these other women of yours when they found your skin had a baby's taste?

JUPITER

No, no,—I don't think so.

MERCURY

With that skin you'd never be allowed a second visit here. And now, Jupiter, please be good enough to contract the sheath of mortality in which you have encased yourself. It's too big for you, you're floating in it.

JUPITER

It's true.

MERCURY

Contract! (*Makes a gesture as with a rapier thrust.*)

JUPITER

(*Flexing muscles in arms until he achieves the position of Christ on the Cross*)

It cramps me! I feel my heart beating against it. My veins bursting! My arteries distending! I feel myself becoming a

53

filter—an hour-glass of blood! The birth of all humanity strains inside me—beating me black and blue! I hope that all my poor human beings don't suffer like this!

MERCURY

Twice they do—once when they're born and once when they die.

JUPITER
(*Straightens up*)

How very disagreeable . . . to experience both simultaneously.

MERCURY

You do not lessen the torture by dividing the process.

JUPITER

Tell me, Mercury, as you stand before me, do you get the impression that you are standing before a man?

MERCURY
(*Eyeing him over*)

No, not yet . . . not quite yet. . . . What I'm chiefly aware of when I stand before the living body of a man is that he is constantly undergoing change—disintegration—and that he incessantly ages. And as I watch the light in his eyes, I see it with the flying instants incessantly growing dimmer and dimmer.

54

JUPITER

Let's try!

MERCURY

What are you going to do?

JUPITER

(*Begins to stoop like an old man*)
I'm saying to myself: "I'm going to die . . . I'm going to die."

MERCURY

No, not so fast . . . you're aging prematurely. Slow the tempo! You're living at the scale at which a dog lives or a cat.

JUPITER

(*Straightens up a little and extends his arm to* MERCURY)
How's this? (*Breathes slower, like a fish.*)

MERCURY

(*Puts his arms, one above and one underneath* JUPITER's *arm*)
No. Now your heartbeats are too widely spaced. You're living now at fish rhythm. You're not, Jupiter, please to remember, a fish. (*By this time* JUPITER *is straight*) There . . . that's it . . . that's it. Keep up that little half-way gallop between the dogs and the fishes. It's this little ambling inner rhythm by which Amphitryon recognizes his horses, and Alkmena the heartbeats of her husband. (JUPITER *looks out front*) What are you thinking?

JUPITER

That I want to be loved for myself alone. I shall make Alkmena accept a lover!

MERCURY

Alkmena, I'm very much afraid, will deny you that pleasure. You better stick to being her husband.

JUPITER

Her husband—and her lover. No woman could resist that. We'll begin that way and later on—we shall see—we shall see— (*Starts to go but* MERCURY *raises hand and stops him*) Any last minute instructions?

MERCURY

Yes. About your intellect.

JUPITER

What's wrong with my intellect?

MERCURY

We must replace all your god-like conceptions with human ones. What are your beliefs? Recite to me your *man's* idea of the nature of this universe.

JUPITER

My *man's* idea of the nature of this universe? I believe that this flat Earth is flat; (MERCURY *picks up helmet gives it*

56

to JUPITER, *who puts it on*) I believe that water is water and nothing else; (MERCURY *picks up shield and hands it to* JUPITER) I believe that air is simple and indivisible; I believe that nature is nature— (MERCURY *picks up spear and hands it to* JUPITER) and the spirit—well, the spirit— In fact, I believe that there is nothing beyond what I can see, and beyond what I can understand. Is that all?

MERCURY

Not quite. Are you consumed by a desire to part your hair in the middle and keep it set that way unalterably with sticky hair lotion?

JUPITER

I feel that temptation—passionately!

MERCURY

Good! Do you conceive that one day you may die?

JUPITER

That I may die? No, never! That my poor friends may die, alas, yes, my poor friends—but not I!

MERCURY

Splendid! Have you forgotten all the women you've already loved?

JUPITER

I've never loved anyone but Alkmena.

MERCURY

And this sky over us—what do you think of this sky?

JUPITER

I believe that the sky is my own personal property. I believe that I possess it far more than I ever did before.

MERCURY

Oh, Jupiter!

JUPITER

And as for the whole solar system, it seems to me very small!

MERCURY

And the whole vast Earth?

JUPITER

Very small! . . . And, Mercury . . . I feel . . . handsomer than Apollo! Braver than Mars . . . more capable of amorous exploits than—myself. And for the first time, Mercury, I really feel myself, I really see myself, I really believe myself, to be master of the gods!

MERCURY

Well, you're a man all right. Get on with it. (*The light in the palace goes out.* JUPITER *makes a motion of knocking on gate, without touching it and there is an accompanying metallic knock heard. There is no reply from the palace. He crosses right and waves the knocks on the gate from where he stands.)*

JUPITER

I know she's there.

MERCURY

How do you know?

JUPITER

She was looking from her window as I came down.

MERCURY

You don't think she recognized you?

JUPITER

No. She thought I was a falling star and wished on me!

MERCURY

You'd better try again. (JUPITER *again makes the motion of knocking on gate and once more the accompanying metallic knock is heard.* MERCURY *waits until he hears* ALKMENA's *voice then stealthily exits.)*

ALKMENA
(Off stage; in Palace)

Who is that knocking? Who disturbs me in my sleep?

JUPITER

(Standing beneath Palace, hiding his face with shield)
A general!

ALKMENA

(Off stage; in Palace)
A general? And what is a general doing wandering about at this time of night? Is he a deserter? Or is he defeated?

JUPITER

Defeated—by love!

ALKMENA

I know only one general and he wouldn't admit such a defeat.

JUPITER

That shows you do not know your own general.

ALKMENA

If I don't know him, how can I admit him?

JUPITER

Because he comes for once as your lover. Let him in!

ALKMENA

(Comes out on balcony)
It is to Alkmena you speak. I have no lover. (JUPITER *laughs derisively*) Why do you laugh?

JUPITER

Did you not only a moment ago open the window of your room and look out, anguished, into the night?

ALKMENA

Yes, I did. But I was looking at the night and that's all I was looking at.

JUPITER

But did you not feel your heart contract and your body expand at the thought of a man, who is, I confess it, extremely ugly and generally rather limited?

ALKMENA

Do you confess it, perhaps, because you wish to be contradicted?

JUPITER

No, not necessarily. And as you gazed up at a falling star, did you not wish aloud: "Oh, if only while he were at the war, I might forego all memory"?

ALKMENA

I might have wished to forget that he loves his horses and his battles better than he loves me. And what does that prove?

JUPITER

That you have a lover, and that he is here.

ALKMENA

I have a husband and he is evidently not here. And I receive no one in my bedroom who is not my husband. And not
even him will I admit if he does not acknowledge his name.
You're not very good at passionate disguises—it's not your
metier.

JUPITER

Oh, at this hour, when everything between here and heaven
is in disguise, may not your husband also disguise himself
as a lover?

ALKMENA

Your insight, my friend, is not very keen if you think the
night is only the day-time masked, the moon no more than
a sun disguised, and that the love of a wife for her husband
can be confused with an amour.

JUPITER

Wifely love is a duty. Duty is compulsion. And compulsion
kills desire.

ALKMENA

Desire! Desire is a half-god. We, here, worship only the
major ones. The lesser gods we leave to adolescent girls, to
the casually married, to the fugitive romantics, the half-wives.

JUPITER

It is blasphemy to speak so even of a lesser god!

ALKMENA

In my secret heart I am more blasphemous even than that
for I worship a god that doesn't exist at all. Shall I tell you
who it is? It's the god of conjugal love, one that it never occurred to the gods to invent—they are so casual. If you come
in behalf of Desire you ask me to betray a greater god for a
lesser. If then you are a lover I am sorry but I must ask you
to go on. . . . You are handsome and you have a good figure.
Your voice is winning. Did it sound in behalf of Fidelity I
might love this voice. I might wish to be enclosed in those
arms. Your mouth, too, I should say, is dewy and ardent. But
I shan't allow it to persuade me. I shall not open my door
to a lover. Who are you?

JUPITER

Why can't your husband be your lover?

ALKMENA

Because a lover is closer always to love than he is to the
object of his love. Because it is ill-bred to deceive your husband—even with himself. Because I like my windows open
and my linen fresh. (*She goes back inside.* MERCURY *enters.*)

JUPITER

She's impossible.

MERCURY

She's set in her ways.

JUPITER

You can't talk to her.

MERCURY

Not in your language.

JUPITER

You can't appeal to her!

MERCURY

She is unfortunately a good woman.

JUPITER

Mercury, she's not a woman, she's a fortress!

MERCURY

A fortress that may be taken only by her husband. Do as I advised you in the first place—be her husband!

JUPITER

Very well—I'll humble myself. (*Gives shield and spear to* MERCURY.)

MERCURY

That's better.

64

JUPITER

But once I am admitted as her husband—then I'll make her yearn for something more.

MERCURY

No doubt. You have your own resources, Jupiter. Meantime—

JUPITER

Meantime— (*Waves* MERCURY *off.* MERCURY *exits as* JUPITER *knocks again.*)

ALKMENA

Who is it now? I seem to have a perfect stream of visitors tonight. Now who are you?

JUPITER

I am Amphitryon, your husband!

ALKMENA

(*Comes in at last*)

Amphitryon! Why didn't you say so in the first place?

JUPITER

Let me in!

ALKMENA

Are you he by whose side I wake every morning and for whom I cut from the margin of my own day an extra ten minutes of sleep?

JUPITER

I am he.

ALKMENA

Are you the one whose least footfall is so familiar to me that I can tell whether he is shaving or dressing?

JUPITER

I am the one.

ALKMENA

Are you the being with whom I dine and breakfast and sup? And whom I allow to go to sleep ten minutes every night before I do?

JUPITER

I am that being.

ALKMENA

Then swear in the presence of the night those marriage vows which hitherto we have spoken only in the presence of the day.

JUPITER

A wedding ceremony, in the void of the night, with neither priest nor altar? What for?

ALKMENA

That the invisible beings which surround us may not be deceived seeing Alkmena receive you like this—like a lover

That the clear light in which we live by day may transfigure even the night. Oh, Amphitryon, I have often dreamed of an occasion like this! Why should the night be the hand-maiden for the clandestine—the furtive—the illicit? Let her for once be bridesmaid to married love. Do you think I wish this lovely night—this constellation of stars and little winds—this company of night moths and shadows—to imagine that I, Alkmena, am receiving a lover? No! At this hour, when there are consummated so many false marriages, let us seal our nocturnal, true one! Shall we begin?

JUPITER

If you only knew, Alkmena, how pitiful to the gods human beings seem, prating their vows, launching their thunderless thunderbolts.

ALKMENA

Raise your hand and crook your index finger! (*Raises her hand and crooks her index finger.*)

JUPITER

No! Not the index finger.

ALKMENA

Why not?

JUPITER

That is the most formidable oath of all. The one used by Jupiter to fester the Earth with plagues.

ALKMENA

The index finger or nothing. If not the index finger, you must go away!

JUPITER

(*Beaten; raises his right arm and crooks index finger at the at the same time, covering right side of his face with mantle*)
Celestial calamities—restrain yourselves! Earthquakes and floods, fevers and locusts—hold off!

ALKMENA

Amphitryon, those are not the words!

JUPITER

I was just practising. (*Lets down mantle and proceeds in earnest*) I, Amphitryon, son and grandson of former generals, father and grandfather of future generals . . . indispensable clasp in the twin girdle of war and glory—

ALKMENA

(*With her right arm also raised and index finger crooked*)
I, Alkmena, whose parents are no longer and whose children are yet unborn—poor isolated link in the chain of humanity—

JUPITER

I swear so to contrive it that the fragrance of the name of Alkmena shall survive so long as the hurly-burly of my own
68

ALKMENA

And I swear to be faithful to Amphitryon, my husband,
or to die!

JUPITER
(*Alarmed*)

To what?

ALKMENA

To die!

JUPITER

Don't say that, Alkmena.

ALKMENA

Why not? I mean it. And now, dear husband, the ceremony is over and I authorize you to come in. You know
you've really been very simple. The gate was open all the
time—you had only to push it—ever so little. . . . (JUPITER
*opens gate, goes up three steps and then stands there as if
rooted to the spot*) Why do you hesitate?

JUPITER

You really mean it? You really *want me* to come in?

ALKMENA

My dearest love . . . I command it! (JUPITER *mounts the
steps quickly, tears the sashes off her, and enfolds her in his
mantle as the curtain falls.*)

ACT TWO

ACT TWO

Scene I

SCENE: *Outside of* ALKMENA'S *bedroom in* AMPHITRYON'S *Palace.*

TIME: *The next morning. The darkness is complete save for the glow of light which emanates from the body of* MERCURY *lying semi-recumbent at the front of the stage.*

MERCURY

Posted here in front of Alkmena's bedroom, I have been soaking in the sweet silence, the gentle resistance, the easy struggle from indoors; already Alkmena bears within herself the young half-god, but never with any other mistress has Jupiter tarried this long—whether this abnormal darkness is beginning to bore you I can not say, but this job that Jupiter has wished on me of prolonging the night till he gets ready to get up is beginning to weigh on me a bit. Especially when I think that everywhere else the whole world is suffused in broad daylight. After all it's midsummer and early in the morning. The great inundation of day canopies out over all the world, thousands and thousands of leagues to the very margin of the sea. Solitary, amid the rose-drenched cubes, this palace is left a cone of black. I really ought to wake my master; he loathes a hurried exit and he will surely wish by way of dressing-gown chatter to reveal to Alkmena that he is Jupiter. He will not willingly forego this sop to his vanity. He will love to enjoy her astonishment and to savor in her pride. Besides, I've suggested to Amphitryon that he come to surprise his wife at break of dawn. This is a courtesy we owe him and it will relieve the situation of any ambiguity. Already, Amphitryon has taken secretly to the road, he is galloping furiously and within the hour he will arrive here at this palace. Therefore, Sun, display your rays to me, that I may choose the one best fitted to kindle these shadows. . . . (*The Sun obliges with a green ray which picks out* MERCURY's *winged boot*) No, no. There's nothing more sinister than green rays for lovers to wake up on. Each one thinks the other has been drowned in the night. . . . (*A purple ray comes on as the green one disappears*) Nor that one. . . . Purple and violet are colors that inflame the senses. We'll save them for tonight. (*The Sun obliges with an amber ray*) Ah, that's it, saffron! Nothing so well as saffron to bring out the insipid quality of the human skin. . . . Get on with it, Sun! (MERCURY *rises and runs off in the darkness. The stage is flooded in full sunlight.*)

ACT TWO

Scene II

SCENE: *A room in the Palace. There is a couch in the center. Two small tabourets one on each side of couch. There is an urn on each tabouret. Also a small handle-bell.*

ALKMENA *enters, puts down her cloak and hat on couch.*

ALKMENA

Get up, Amphitryon, the sun has risen.

JUPITER
(*Off stage*)

Where am I?

ALKMENA

In the last place where husbands think they are when they wake up; simply in your own home in your own bed, and with your own wife. (*Rings bell.*)

JUPITER
(*Still off stage*)
And what is the name of this wife?

ALKMENA

Her name is the same by day as it is by night—it is still
Alkmena.

JUPITER

Is it that marvellousıy dark Alkmena—who never says a
word while love-making?

ALKMENA

Yes, and who prattles of dawn, and who is now about to
put you out of here, husband or no husband. Come along,
Amphitryon, you'll be late for your war! Are you getting
dressed?

JUPITER
(*Still off stage*)
Yes. Oh, come back to my arms!

ALKMENA

Don't count on that! Dark women have this in common
with dreams—you may embrace them only at night.

JUPITER

Well, come back and close your eyes then and let us make
the best of an improvised darkness.

ALKMENA

No, no, the early morning is no time for improvisation. Get
up, Amphitryon. Please. (*Sits on couch, her feet stretched out*)
Come along, darling, breakfast is ready. (KLEANTHA *and*

76

NENETZA, *two maids, come in with breakfast trays.* NENETZA *serves* ALKMENA. KLEANTHA *stands holding her tray.* JUPITER *enters and as he passes* ALKMENA, *she fondly slaps his behind and he stops a moment and smiles with satisfaction. Sits at end of couch, his feet outstretched.* KLEANTHA *puts tray on his lap and then both maids exit.*)

JUPITER

What a divine night!

ALKMENA

Your adjectives this morning, darling, are somewhat feeble.

JUPITER

I said divine!

ALKMENA

You could say a cut of beef was divine or a meal was divine, but for last night you might have found something better.

JUPITER

What could there possibly be better?

ALKMENA

Almost any adjective except divine. It's such a worn-out word. Perfect! You could have said it was a perfect night. Charming! Best of all, you might have said it was a pleasant night! Now, that conveys so many agreeable sensations: *"What a pleasant night!"*

77

JUPITER

But don't you think that this night, of all our nights, was the pleasantest, by far?

ALKMENA
(*Drinking*)

Well, that depends.

JUPITER

On what does it depend?

ALKMENA

Have you forgotten, my own husband, the night we were married? The miraculous discovery our two hearts made of each other, in the midst of those shadows which for the first time held us in their embrace? That was our most beautiful night!

JUPITER

Our most beautiful, yes. But the pleasantest was this one.

ALKMENA
(*Nonchalantly*)

Do you think so?

JUPITER

Yes, I do.

ALKMENA

I don't. What about the night the great fire broke out in Thebes—and you came back to me at sunrise all gilt from the fire and warm as new-baked bread? That was our pleasantest night and you'll never persuade me differently. (*Eats fruit.*)

JUPITER

Well, if nothing else, then, you must admit this was the most astonishing.

ALKMENA

Was it? Why? Now, the night before last, for instance, when you rescued that little drowning boy from the sea, and all night long you kept flinging your arms around me to rescue me from imaginary drowning—yes, that was rather astonishing, if you like. No, my dear, if you wish to sum up this night in an appropriate adjective, I should say that this night, of all our nights, was the most—connubial. That's it, my sweet —connubial! There was a sense of security about it which gladdened me. Never have I felt so certain of waking up in the morning to find you beside me; there was mercifully absent that fear which obsesses me constantly—of finding you suddenly dead in my arms. (*Eats the fruit.*)

JUPITER

(*Puts the tray down with sudden distaste*)
Connubial—? (*Sits up with feet on floor.*)

ALKMENA

Connubial!

JUPITER
(Rises)

Lovely room!

ALKMENA

It seems especially attractive to you this morning when you have no business to be here.

JUPITER

How clever of men, to devise this system of colonnades which seems to intensify the light in a planet relatively so badly lit.

ALKMENA

Since it was you who devised the system, darling, that's very modest of you.

JUPITER

Beautiful landscape!

ALKMENA

Ah, that you may admire since you did not create it.

JUPITER
(Significantly)

And who did, may I ask?

ALKMENA
(Nonchalantly)

The Master of the Gods.

80

JUPITER

And may one hear his name?

ALKMENA

Jupiter.

JUPITER
(*Ravished, leans over couch*)

How prettily you pronounce the names of the gods! Who taught you to savor them so on your lips, as if you were enjoying a heavenly diet? Like a lamb that nibbles at laburnum and lifts his head to nibble more. Say his name again—repeat his name! It is said that the gods, summoned so, respond sometimes with their very presence!

ALKMENA
(*Calling*)

Neptune! Apollo!

JUPITER

No, no, the first one—repeat his name.

ALKMENA

No, no, no. I like to nibble all over Olympus. Especially I love to pronounce the names of the gods in couples: (*Calling*) Venus and Mars! Jupiter and Juno!

JUPITER
(*Laughs nervously*)

No, no, no.

81

ALKMENA

I see them wandering about eternally—hand in hand—on the crests of the clouds—it must be marvelous!

JUPITER

Great fun! You think that Jupiter has done a good job then, with these rocks and cliffs—he's done pretty well on this landscape?

ALKMENA

Yes, it's very nice, but do you think he did it on purpose?

JUPITER
(*Shocked*)

Alkmena!

ALKMENA

Well, everything you do, you do on purpose, whether you are grafting cherry trees on plums or contriving a double edged sword. But do you think that Jupiter, on the day that he created all this, knew what he was doing?

JUPITER
(*Hurt*)

It is generally assumed that he did!

ALKMENA

We know he created the Earth. But the beauty of the Earth re-creates itself momentarily. Jupiter seems too settled to have dallied so with the ephemeral!

82

JUPITER

I'm afraid you haven't a very precise idea of the purpose of creation.

ALKMENA

No, I suppose I haven't. How does it all seem to you, darling? Doesn't it seem cloudy?

JUPITER

No, no! I see everything perfectly clearly. (*Sits beside her again*) In the beginning everything was Chaos. It was then Jupiter's felicitous idea to separate everything into four elements.

ALKMENA

We have only four elements?

JUPITER

Four. And the first is water, and water, I may tell you, was not so easy to create. Superficially, water looks like quite ordinary stuff. But imagine, if you had never seen water—if there were no water in existence, what it would mean to create it—even to get the idea of creating it.

ALKMENA

What did the goddesses cry—in the pre-water era? Bronze tears? That stumps you!

JUPITER

Don't interrupt me, Alkmena, I'm trying to give you some idea of what Jupiter must be—I'm trying to convey to you

83

something of his scope. He may materialize before you at an
moment, you know, without warning. Wouldn't you like t
have him explain everything to you personally in all hi
magnificence? (*He gets up.*)

ALKMENA

No, darling, I'd rather have you explain it to me.

JUPITER
(*Nonplussed, sits again*)
Where was I?

ALKMENA

We've just disposed of original Chaos.

JUPITER

Oh, yes. Once water was in existence it occurred to him t
bank it in with broken coasts, in order to stop the impact o
the storms, and to strew the surface of the waters with Con
tinents, in order to spare the eyes of the gods the perpetua
irritation of a glittering horizon— And so came the Eart
and all its marvels!

ALKMENA

Oh, you mean the pine trees?

JUPITER

Pine trees?

ALKMENA

And the echo?

84

JUPITER

The echo?

ALKMENA

You sound like one yourself. Now color—did Jupiter create color?

JUPITER
(*Proudly*)

Yes. The seven colors of the rainbow are his invention.

ALKMENA

No, no—I mean my favorite colors: bronze and dark red and lizard green—what of them?

JUPITER

No, he left those to the cleaning and dyeing establishments—

ALKMENA
(*Notices a hole in his sock*)

Amphitryon! You have a hole in your stocking—did Jupiter create that?

JUPITER
(*Pleased at his own verisimilitude*)

Yes—!

ALKMENA

Oh, he did, did he? (*Calling*) Nenetza! Yarn, yarn:

JUPITER

Shall we go back to the assorted vibrations in the ether, of which I was speaking— (NENETZA *enters with yarn and sewing stand and places it near couch.* ALKMENA *picks a needle and proceeds to mend the sock.* NENETZA *takes both breakfast trays and goes out.*)

ALKMENA

Yes, yes— You can't go to war with a hole in your stocking. What will your enemy think of your wife? Give it to me. (*Takes the sock off his foot.*)

JUPITER

But to go back again to the assorted vibrations in the ether— (ALKMENA *sews placidly*) Jupiter so contrived it, that by a system of molecular collision—infinite impacts and double impacts within the molecules—as well as counter-refraction of the original light refractions he was able to criss-cross the Universe with a network of a thousand different systems of color and sound, at once perceptible or not to human sense organs—

ALKMENA

That's exactly what I was saying.

JUPITER

What *you* were saying?

ALKMENA

Yes. He didn't do a thing! He didn't do a thing except plunge us into an awful conglomeration of illusions and

86

stupors from which we have to extricate ourselves—I and my dear husband. (*She pinches the big toe of his bare foot.*)

JUPITER

Alkmena, are you aware that the gods may be eavesdropping?

ALKMENA

Oh, they know my heart is straightforward and honest. Besides, what does Jupiter expect of me? That I should expire with gratitude to him for having invented four elements when we could very well use twenty? I don't think four elements is much, considering he hasn't had anything else to do for all eternity. I am far more grateful to you, my dear husband, and my heart bursts with gratitude to you for having invented a system of window-pulleys which has lightened my life and for all those wonderful, new graftings you did for the orchard. (*She puts the mended sock on his foot*) You, Amphitryon, have changed for me the taste of a cherry— (*Puts his sandal on*) and you have done more than that—you have enlarged the capacity of my pantry shelves! Now, for me, it is you who are the creator— (JUPITER *is staring at her with divine admiration*) Why do you look at me like that? Compliments embarrass you, is that it? I suppose you find me too earthbound?

JUPITER

(*Bends down and kisses her feet*)
Wouldn't you like to be less so?

ALKMENA

Less so?

JUPITER

You never aspired to be a goddess?

ALKMENA

A goddess? What on earth for?

JUPITER

To be honored and revered by everyone.

ALKMENA

Certainly not!

JUPITER

To be able to walk on water and on the air—

ALKMENA

No, darling, no.

JUPITER

To understand the meaning of things and other worlds?

ALKMENA

No. I've never taken an undue interest in my neighbors.

JUPITER

Why—then—to be immortal!

ALKMENA

To be immortal? What for? What good would that do me?

JUPITER

Not to die!

ALKMENA

Not to die! What would I do if I didn't die?

JUPITER

Dearest Alkmena! You would be changed into a star. You would live forever. You would shine in the night till the end of time.

ALKMENA

The end of time? And when will that take place?

JUPITER

Never!

ALKMENA

Oh, dear, what a long evening! No, darling, no. For that job of night watchwoman the gods had better not count on me. (*Sits up*) Besides, the night air isn't good for my skin. Wouldn't I get all chapped up there in the trough of eternity?

JUPITER

(*Moves along couch beside her*)

But—oh, my darling—how cold and empty you'd be in the trough of death! (*He buries his head in her bosom.*)

ALKMENA

Oh, sweet. I'm not afraid of death. It's the stake you give for life. I prefer to identify myself with my own companions, who must also die. I feel so strongly that my very fibres will perpetuate themselves in other men—and animals—plants even—that I should feel cheated if I were not allowed to follow this mysterious destiny. Don't talk to me of not dying, so long as there is a vegetable alive which isn't immortal. For a human being to be immortal—is a kind of betrayal of one's own. Besides, when I think of the wonderful surcease death brings; to be irritated for sixty years over meals that don't turn out well—holes in stockings—aches and pains—and then to be offered death—the felicity of death—really, it's a reward we don't deserve!

JUPITER

But wouldn't you like to have a son—an immortal son?

ALKMENA

To want one's son to be immortal is only human.

JUPITER

One who would become the greatest of heroes! One who as a baby would slay serpents come to strangle him in his crib.

ALKMENA

No, certainly not. He'll be just a little baby who will coo and be frightened of flies. What are you so upset about?

JUPITER

Alkmena, did you really mean it, when you said you'd rather kill yourself than be unfaithful?

ALKMENA

Darling, can you doubt it?

JUPITER

But—to kill one's self is so—dangerous!

ALKMENA

Not for me. If the gods of war should strike you down there wouldn't be anything in the least tragic about my dying.

JUPITER

But suppose you drag to death a child conceived the day before and half alive?

ALKMENA

For him it would be only a half death. He'd be that much ahead on his future.

JUPITER

Alkmena, I can see that you are pious and that you comprehend the mysteries of this world. I must, therefore, speak to you of—

ALKMENA

(*Edging away from him as he tries to embrace her*)

No. I know what that solemn manner of yours leads to. It's your way of being tender. Can't you for once try being intimate without being—pontifical?

JUPITER

You mustn't joke, Alkmena. The time has come when I must speak to you of the gods.

ALKMENA

The gods?

JUPITER

The moment has arrived when I must clarify for you their relations with men.

ALKMENA

(*Rises*)

Have you lost your senses, Amphitryon? You choose this moment of all moments to talk theology to me. At this time of day, when everybody—drunk with sunlight—just can't wait to go farming or fishing!

JUPITER

Alkmena—

ALKMENA

What's more, isn't the army waiting for you? You have only a few minutes left if you want to kill anybody at all— and you'll have to do that on an empty stomach. No, darling, no. (*Goes upstage and gets scarf*) I have my house to attend to—I have my rounds to make—I have the gardener to see— do you think this house runs itself?

92

JUPITER
(*Rises*)

Alkmena! Dearest Alkmena. Let me apprise you that the gods may appear precisely at the moment when you expect them least!

ALKMENA

Amphitryon, dear Amphitryon, in a moment I shall deliver you an harangue, not about the gods, but about my servant problems. (*Comes downstage and picks up her hat and sits beside* JUPITER) As a matter of fact, I very much fear that we shall have to dispense with the services of Nenetza. For apart from her special mania for scrubbing only the black tiles in the mosaics, she has yielded, as you might say, to the gods—and is just a little—pregnant! (*Rises, jauntily puts on her hat*) Till tonight, darling, good-bye— (*Exits.*)

JUPITER
Alkmena— (MERCURY *enters.*)

MERCURY

Jupiter, what's the matter? What's happened? I've been waiting to see you emerge from this room in all your glory as you've done from so many others. Instead, it's Alkmena who makes her departure—not the least bit ruffled.

JUPITER
She isn't ruffled. You can't ruffle her.

MERCURY

This isn't true to form, Jupiter. And what's that vertical crease doing between your eyes? Has somebody upset you? Are you annoyed? Is there going to be thunder?

JUPITER

No. This crease, my dear Mercury, is a wrinkle.

MERCURY

But Jupiter can't have wrinkles. That belongs to Amphitryon.

JUPITER

No—no. This wrinkle belongs to me, it's my wrinkle. (*Looks off after* ALKMENA) And now I know how men come by them.

MERCURY

I've never seen you like this, you're actually stooping with fatigue.

JUPITER

It's no light weight to carry a wrinkle.

MERCURY

Can it be that you have experienced the emotion of human love so thoroughly that it's exhausted you.

JUPITER

I believe that it is love itself I am experiencing.

94

MERCURY

Jupiter, you have the naïveté of the superman. Don't be juvenile, this is hardly your first affair.

JUPITER

But for the first time I held in my arms a woman whom I could not see, whom I could not hear—and yet I understood her.

MERCURY

What went on in your mind?

JUPITER

Only that I was her husband. I had limited the compass of my mind to his.

MERCURY

She never suspected then?

JUPITER

Never! And moreover, and this is strange, I couldn't have endured it if she did. From the moment we went to bed to the moment we got up it was impossible for me to be anything but her husband. It was Alkmena who was completely victorious over me. Do you know, that a few moments ago I had occasion to explain Creation to her and I found myself talking as dry as dust. The easy eloquence of which I am master when I talk to you just—just—dried up— (*Buries his head in his hand in despair*) Mercury, may I expound Creation for you—just to keep my hand in?

MERCURY

If it's absolutely necessary—but just Creation—that's as far as I'll go.

JUPITER

Mercury—I have also made a discovery—

MERCURY

Let me remind you, as you're omniscient, discovery for you is impossible.

JUPITER

Nevertheless, I have discovered that human beings are not what the gods think them. Alkmena, the gentle—the tender Alkmena has the character of a rock. She is the true Prometheus!

MERCURY

It isn't that she has character, she lacks imagination.

JUPITER

Yes, she lacks imagination and it's even possible that she isn't very intelligent. She is ambitious neither to shock nor to dazzle. But it's exactly this single-minded quality in her, this quality of constancy and devotion, against which our power is futile.

MERCURY

Do I hear aright? Is this the Master of the Gods talking?

JUPITER

She is the only woman I have ever met who is as adorable dressed as unveiled, who when she is absent, makes herself felt as if she were present, whose homespun occupations seem to me as alluring as pleasure itself. To dine with her—even to breakfast with her—to touch her hand accidentally with a plate or a spoon— And then suddenly she will use little expressions—and that widens the abyss between us—

MERCURY

What expressions?

JUPITER

She will say—"When I was a child"—or "When I'm old"—or—"Never in all my life"— This stabs me, Mercury.

MERCURY

I don't see why.

JUPITER

We can't use these expressions—

MERCURY

We can say anything we like.

JUPITER

No, we can't—because we are not born and we do not die. It is between these margins that mortals live as they do between the lovely hedges on their country estates. We merely coexist.

MERCURY

But would you exchange a cul-de-sac for a panorama?

JUPITER

With her, Mercury—yes.

MERCURY

To have what every living thing has—it's a commonplace desire, Jupiter.

JUPITER

But we miss something, Mercury—undoubtedly we miss something—the poignance of the transient—the intimation of mortality—that sweet sadness of grasping at something you cannot hold—

MERCURY

It's very simple—make Alkmena immortal!

JUPITER

And deprive her of her death? She'd never forgive me, she'd never forgive me for betraying her to the vegetables. The vegetables would never forgive her. No, I'm too fond of her —and I may tell you now that her son, of all my sons, will be my most favorite.

MERCURY

That the Universe knows already!

JUPITER

The Universe? No one knows anything about this affair.

MERCURY

Oh, yes, they do. I announced everything this morning! (JUPITER *rises angrily, raises his right arm and his index finger crooked. A rumbling of thunder obeys his gesture and* MERCURY *drops to one knee in terror*) I only did what I've always done in all your affairs. Why should we suddenly conceal from the world how generous you are?

JUPITER

Did you announce that I had visited Alkmena disguised as Amphitryon?

MERCURY

Certainly not! There's something undignified about that trick. I was afraid it might make a bad impression and since your desire to spend another evening with Alkmena was so obvious that I could sense it through the very walls, I made the formal announcement that Alkmena would receive a visit from Jupiter tonight!

JUPITER

To whom did you announce this?

MERCURY

In the order prescribed by destiny! (*A cosmic music is heard*) First to the winds, then to the waters: listen, the undulations of the Universe, both wet and dry, are gossiping in their special language of nothing else.

99

JUPITER

We're lost! Poor Alkmena, we're lost! (MERCURY *rises*) She would never allow it. (*Sits on couch again*) She'd kill herself! And Hercules, my son, would die also. And I would be forced, as I was when I had you, to open my thigh or the fatty part of my calf to shelter a foetus for several months. (*Gong is heard*) No, thank you very much. What's that?

MERCURY

(*Goes up to Arch and looks off*)

It's the whole of Thebes preparing to celebrate your union with Alkmena. They're organizing a procession.

JUPITER

Turn it back! Let the sea engulf it!

MERCURY

Jupiter, that's impossible, these are your own priests.

JUPITER

They have insufficient reasons for their faith in me. (*Gong stops*) For the first time, Mercury, I have a suspicion that a thoroughly first-rate god might make a thoroughly second-rate man. (*Music again*) What's that?

MERCURY

It's the Virgins coming to congratulate Alkmena—in their theoretical way.

JUPITER

Don't you think it would be a good idea to drown the Virgins and strike down the priests?

MERCURY

It depends on what you're after fundamentally. What do you want?

JUPITER

What do I want? What every man wants! A thousand contradictory desires! That Alkmena should remain faithful to her husband and also give herself to me. That she should remain chaste under my caresses and yet that desire should flame up in her under my very sight. That she should know nothing of this intrigue and yet that she should connive at it with all her might!

MERCURY

I've done my stint. The Universe is informed according to prescription that tonight Alkmena will receive a visit from Jupiter. Is there anything else that I can do for you? (*Drops to one knee before* JUPITER.)

JUPITER

Yes! See that she does it—and willingly. It is no longer a question of my son, that matter is fortunately disposed of. It is now a question of ME! Of I, myself! I'm degraded by this mortal livery. I shall come to her as a god! (*Rises majestically.*

Music) You must see her—prepare her for my visit—outline vividly my love for her. I permit you to approach her, to touch her, agitate her blood, her nerves, appeal to her pride.

MERCURY
(*Rises*)

That's the spirit, Jupiter. Now that you are willing to forego your incognito I may tell you I'll persuade her in an instant. She'll be waiting for you, I promise you.

ALKMENA
(*Calling off stage*)

Darling!

ECHO
(*Calling off stage*)

Darling!

JUPITER

Whom is she talking to?

MERCURY

She's flirting with Amphitryon through her echo—and you say she isn't a coquette! Even for her voice she has a mirror!

ALKMENA
(*Calling off stage*)

Darling!

ECHO
(*Calling off stage*)

Darling! (*Music.*)

JUPITER

"Nymph, in thy orisons, be all thy sins remembered. . . ."
What are you smiling at?

MERCURY

Have you heard that expression somewhere before?

JUPITER

No, somewhere not yet. It is whispered to me in the future,
by a poet yet unborn. I warn you, I shall not leave this city
until she has capitulated in my honor of her own free will!
(*Music.*)

ALKMENA
(*Calling off stage*)

Darling!

ECHO
(*Calling off stage*)

Darling! (JUPITER *exits.* MERCURY *conceals himself.* ALKMENA
enters, followed by KLEANTHA, *bearing a garden basket full of
vegetables and* ALKMENA'S *hat.*)

ALKMENA

Kleantha, will you look at those turnips! Your master
doesn't like turnips, but when they're cooked, he thinks they're
something else. And tell cook to fan those melons until they're
cool, if she has to fan all day.

KLEANTHA

Yes, mistress. (*Exits with sewing stand, basket and hat.* MERCURY *comes down from his hiding place.*)

MERCURY

'Salutations, Princess!

ALKMENA

(*Amazed, stops at arch*)

You're a god!

MERCURY

Not of the first rank—but a god.

ALKMENA

You're Mercury. I know your face.

MERCURY

Thank you, Princess. Most people recognize me by my feet—by the wings on my feet. If you care to touch me, I'm in a position to authorize it. (*She curtsies to him*) I see the gods interest you.

ALKMENA

Oh, I love the gods.

MERCURY

All of them? Am I included in this affection?

ALKMENA

You're one of my favorites.

104

MERCURY

Why?

ALKMENA

Your name—Mercury—is so beautiful. Then—of course, you are the god of eloquence. I knew that the moment I saw you.

MERCURY

Your face, too, Princess, is a kind of exquisite speech. (MERCURY *graciously indicates that she may sit. She does so*) But tell me—have you no preference among the gods?

ALKMENA

Of course I have a preference—Jupiter!

MERCURY

Jupiter? You astonish me rather. He has no specialty.

ALKMENA

Isn't divinity a kind of specialty?

MERCURY

Yes, but he isn't gifted. Are you so influenced by his position as Master of the Gods? It's a kind of snobbery I wouldn't have expected from you.

ALKMENA

He's very beautiful.

105

MERCURY

He has no knowledge of rhetoric.

ALKMENA

No?

MERCURY

And no connoisseurship in the fine arts.

ALKMENA

But he's so dignified!

MERCURY

Musically he's tone deaf. He can't distinguish between celestial and chamber music. We must face it, Alkmena, Jupiter is not talented.

ALKMENA

If you'll forgive my saying so, Mercury, I think you're being a little disloyal to your master? Why, only a few moments ago, my husband and I were saying how wonderful he is with . . . molecules.

MERCURY

Yes, but he's mad about women.

ALKMENA

I understand these passionate impulses of his which cause him to hurl himself into the arms of mortal women. You see, I've learned from my husband all about grafting—he's done wonderful things with cherries, you know. You must have heard of him up there.

106

MERCURY

Oh, of course.

ALKMENA

Yes, of course. Then, at school, we used to recite poems about the gods making crossings with beauty and even with purity that got the most wonderful results when performed with women especially honored for this high mission— Does this bore you?

MERCURY

No, on the contrary, you fill me with delight. The fate, then, of all the women whom Jupiter's loved or ever will love seems to you a happy fate?

ALKMENA

Infinitely happy.

MERCURY

Enviable?

ALKMENA

Highly enviable.

MERCURY

In short—you envy them?

ALKMENA

I envy them. Why do you ask me that?

MERCURY

Don't you guess why? Don't you know why I've come here
and what announcement I have to make to you as a special
messenger from my master?

ALKMENA

No. Tell me.

MERCURY

It's that he loves you. Jupiter loves you.

ALKMENA

Jupiter—loves me? Oh— (*Laughs at the preposterousness of
the idea*) I am the most fortunate of women.

MERCURY

He's had his eye on you for a number of days now. Not
one of your gestures has been wasted on him. You are in-
effably traced in his radiant vision.

ALKMENA

For a number of days?

MERCURY

And a number of nights. (*Notices her shocked expression*)
You grow pale—

ALKMENA

I know I should blush . . . but it kills me to think that
Jupiter's been looking at me all this time and I probably wasn't
at my best. Why didn't you warn me?

108

MERCURY

And what answer shall I give him now?

ALKMENA

(*Rises, as does* MERCURY)

Tell him—of course—that I shall do my best to earn his gracious favor. I already have a silver altar to him in the Palace. When Amphitryon returns, we'll build a gold one.

MERCURY

It isn't an altar he's interested in.

ALKMENA

Everything here belongs to him. Even my most precious possessions. He has only to choose.

MERCURY

He's already chosen it and tonight he's coming to claim it.

ALKMENA

What is it?

MERCURY

Your bed. I have just given my orders to the night. The day is hardly long enough for the night to get together the brilliant effects and the appropriate sounds for a celestial wedding. It will be less a night than a sample of your immortal future. It gives me pleasure to season your more perishable moments with these pinches of immortality—my engagement present! (ALKMENA *smiles*) Why do you smile?

109

ALKMENA

I've smiled at less.

MERCURY

But why?

ALKMENA

Quite simply because this is obviously a case of mistaken identity. I am Alkmena, and Amphitryon is my husband.

MERCURY

But the cosmic forces do not consider husbands.

ALKMENA

But think, Mercury, of all women in Thebes, to have chosen me? I'm a very commonplace woman. I wasn't very good at school and what I did learn I've forgotten. I am not, in fact, considered over bright.

MERCURY

That opinion I do not share.

ALKMENA

At the moment it's not you I'm thinking of, but Jupiter. When it comes to a momentous matter—like receiving Jupiter —I'm simply not up to it.

MERCURY

We've seen you from on high and your body lights up the night of Greece.

ALKMENA

Yes, I have my devices for artificial lighting—I have my powders and lotions—I manage with tweezers and files to put up some kind of an appearance, but I cannot write and I cannot even think.

MERCURY

But you talk very well. Even if you didn't, it wouldn't matter because tonight all the poets of posterity will be carrying on the conversation for you.

ALKMENA

I wish they'd carry the rest as well.

MERCURY

This flippancy doesn't become you, Alkmena. Do you think you can escape the gods by underestimating your surpassing qualities of nobility and beauty? Besides you seem to be unaware of the magnificence of this—opportunity.

ALKMENA

But that's exactly what I'm trying to convey to you, Mercury—how little I am suited for this opportunity. I live in the earthiest of atmospheres. It is so thick that no god could stand it—not for long—

MERCURY

You are overestimating the time. This isn't a liaison. It's a matter of a few hours.

III

ALKMENA

How do you know? Jupiter may turn out to be constant. That he should be interested at all is what I can't get over.

MERCURY

I don't see why. You will admit your figure is superlative.

ALKMENA

My figure is all right, but does Jupiter know that I tan the most dreadful color in summer?

MERCURY

Your hands embellish the flowers as you pick them in your garden.

ALKMENA

My hands are all right but one has only two hands, and I'll tell you something, Mercury, that isn't generally known—I have one tooth too many.

MERCURY

Your walk, though, overflows with promise.

ALKMENA

That's a false lead, believe me. When it comes to love-making, I'm not very mature.

MERCURY

It's no use. Jupiter has observed you in that capacity also.

ALKMENA

(*Starts to cry*)

Sometimes one pretends. . . .

MERCURY

What's this, Alkmena? Do I see tears? (*Music*) At this moment you weep; at this moment when a flood of joy is about to inundate humanity in your honor? Tonight a year of joy begins for Thebes. No more epidemics. No more pestilence. No more war. No more famines.

ALKMENA

It's not fair!

MERCURY

In your city are eight little children who, this very week, were destined to die. Four little boys and four little girls— among the latter your favorite Charissa. You can save them!

ALKMENA

Charissa! . . . If anyone else did this it would be called blackmail!

MERCURY

Health and happiness are the exclusive blackmail of the gods. Do you hear, Alkmena? The poor and the sick are beside themselves with joy for they will owe to you their happiness and their life. Now, Alkmena, you are apprised of what is to be. Farewell!

ALKMENA

You are going?

MERCURY

I must. I have to tell Jupiter you are expecting him.

ALKMENA

You would be telling him a lie. I am not expecting him!

MERCURY

What?

ALKMENA

I am not expecting him.

MERCURY

Why not?

ALKMENA

I am tired. I am ill.

MERCURY

It's not true. Don't try to put off the gods with lies which are effective with men.

ALKMENA

But it is a man I love.

MERCURY

What man?

114

ALKMENA

My husband.

MERCURY

Yes, you love your husband.

ALKMENA

I love him.

MERCURY

But that's what we're counting on! Jupiter doesn't choose his mistresses among unfaithful wives.

ALKMENA

If I am taken by surprise, Mercury, I warn you I shall defend myself if I have only my naked body and my naked legs.

MERCURY

Don't force me to speak bluntly to you, Alkmena, and to reveal to you the hidden depths of what you are pleased to think of as your purity. Conversationally, I find you cynical enough.

ALKMENA

I adapt my speech to yours. You leave me no choice.

MERCURY

Very well, we'll come straight to the point. (*On his knees before her*) From tonight's encounter, a child is to be born.

ALKMENA

The child is already named, I suppose?

MERCURY

Yes. It has a name.

ALKMENA

Poor little girl. She'll never be born.

MERCURY

It's a boy and he will be born!

ALKMENA

What will happen when I refuse?

MERCURY

The child must be born.

ALKMENA

When I kill myself?

MERCURY

Jupiter will reincarnate you for this son must be born.

ALKMENA

A child born of adultery, never! Divine son though he be—
he shall die!

MERCURY

Alkmena, the patience of the gods has its limits. You abuse
their courtesy. After all, we don't need your consent.

SOSIE

(Off stage)

Mistress . . .

ALKMENA

What is it, Sosie?

SOSIE

Queen Leda has just arrived at the Palace.

ALKMENA

Queen Leda?

MERCURY

Leda, the Queen of Sparts, whom Jupiter loved in the guise of a swan, your predecessor. See her, Alkmena; draw her out. She may give you some useful advice.

ALKMENA

I will.

MERCURY

I'm going— I must report our conversation to Jupiter.

ALKMENA

Shall you give him my answer?

MERCURY

I can't believe, Alkmena, that you really want to see your city infected by pestilence, razed to the ground by fire. Do you want to see your husband defeated? I shall tell Jupiter that you're expecting him.

ALKMENA
You'll be telling him a lie!

MERCURY
With women I find the morning lie becomes the evening truth! Till tonight, Alkmena. (MERCURY *exits*.)

ALKMENA
(*Calls*)
Sosie— (SOSIE *enters*) Tell me—Queen Leda—how does she seem?

SOSIE
She's wearing silver piped in swansdown but very good taste.

ALKMENA
No—her face I mean— Haughty? Hard?

SOSIE
No, serene and noble.

ALKMENA
Good! Tell her to come in! (SOSIE *exits*) I have an idea, a wonderful idea. (QUEEN LEDA *comes in. She goes at once to* ALKMENA *and offers her her hand to kiss.* ALKMENA *curtsies befor her and kisses her hand.*)

LEDA
Alkmena, I hope you do not find my visit *too* indiscreet?
118

ALKMENA

No, no, Leda—

LEDA

I was passing through Thebes and heard the news and I wanted to see you.

ALKMENA

I'm enchanted.

LEDA

(*Pointing toward the bedroom and gushing rather*)
Is that the historic bedroom to be?

ALKMENA

It's my bedroom.

LEDA

And is it for tonight?

ALKMENA

I hear it's for tonight.

LEDA

You've done very well, very well indeed. How did you manage it? (*Both sit on couch*) Did you offer endless prayers? Did you cry aloud your misery, your nostalgia for a god?

ALKMENA

No, I expressed my happiness and my contentment.

LEDA

I see—well, perhaps that's an even better way of calling for help. Have you seen him?

ALKMENA

No. Is it he who sends you here?

LEDA

No—

ALKMENA

It's not that you'd like to catch another glimpse of him, is it?

LEDA

Another glimpse? I've never had one. I've never seen him.

ALKMENA

Never?

LEDA

Never!

ALKMENA

I thought you had at least a nodding acquaintance with him.

LEDA

You don't seem to know the details of our little adventure.

ALKMENA

Not intimately—

LEDA

Oh, well—it was summer. (*Music*) Great schools of swan had been coursing high up among the stars. They were so beautiful I couldn't take my eyes off them. My husband even noticed it and made jokes about it—your swan-song will be with a swan, he said.

ALKMENA

Your husband made jokes about it?

LEDA

My husband's an atheist. Not believing in the gods, he sees nothing in this but a vehicle for puns. Of course there is an advantage in that!

ALKMENA

Then it's true what legend tells us, that Jupiter came to you in the guise of a swan?

LEDA

Well—up to a certain point he was, a sort of cloudburst—a gust of swan.

ALKMENA

Was it real down?

Certainly. I touched the wingroots with my fingers—a harp of feathers. Alkmena, to be perfectly frank—I would rather, if you don't mind, that with you he wouldn't be a swan again. I'm not of a jealous disposition at all, but if you could leave me this little distinction, it would be so nice of you. After all, there are so many other birds, much rarer ones, even.

ALKMENA

Yes, but few are as noble and I don't think they're a bit more stupid than geese or eagles, and they sing too, after a fashion, don't they?

LEDA

Oh, indeed they do!

ALKMENA

Nobody listens to them, but they sing. Did he sing?

LEDA

Well—he didn't exactly sing—it was a beautifully enunciated chirp, a chirp of which the sense escaped me but of which the syntax was so pure, the diction so exquisite, that you could just feel the verbs and relative pronouns of bird language.

ALKMENA

Did he overwhelm you—I mean were you taken by surprise?

LEDA

Warned and surprised. Assaulted, gently assaulted. Swathed in a movement which was not earthly but astral, cradled in an eternal cosmic rolling.

ALKMENA

And how did he leave you? Tell me that.

122

LEDA

He rose straight to my zenith. He was gracious enough to endow me for several seconds with his sight. This enabled me to follow him from my zenith to his, from zenith to zenith —and there I lost him.

ALKMENA

Oh, is that all?

LEDA

Well, for the Master of the Gods I think it's a good deal!

ALKMENA

Yes, but after a little while—the next day perhaps—no trifling gift?

LEDA

No.

ALKMENA

No flowers?

LEDA

No.

ALKMENA

Not even a little colored egg?

LEDA

In a way I get little communications from him. The branches of a pear tree, for example, bow down to me in homage as I pass.

ALKMENA

Still, Leda, that's not much, is it?

LEDA

As a matter of fact, I wouldn't have cared for a prolonged liaison even with a god.

ALKMENA

A prolonged liaison, no. But I do think he might have paid you a second visit.

LEDA
(*Crestfallen*)

Do you?

ALKMENA

Yes. Leda, you're not happy. I can tell. Jupiter hasn't made you happy.

LEDA

I am more than happy. I am sanctified.

ALKMENA

You're too young, no, no, you're too beautiful to be canonized so early. It was a shabby trick. Jupiter loved you and abandoned you.

LEDA

Abandoned me?

ALKMENA

Yes, he deserted you, didn't he? He didn't come back, did he? Trying to make it up to you with genuflections from a pear tree! If I were you, Leda, I'd revenge myself. He didn't even make an honest legend of you.

LEDA

How can I revenge myself on a white swan?

ALKMENA

I'll tell you how. With a black one. Substitute for me.

LEDA

What?

ALKMENA

That door leads to my room. You go in there—put on my veils, spray my scent about—I can make it very dark. Jupiter will be deceived and to his advantage.

LEDA

But you don't know, you don't realize what it means. If you knew him as I do, you wouldn't be so generous.

ALKMENA

I thought you said you didn't know him.

LEDA

I know him as a bird! Alkmena, in spite of everything I've said, it was worth it! You'll see, you'll be so relaxed.

125

ALKMENA

But I don't want to be relaxed, I'm not a bit tense. And besides I've already made up my mind to refuse him.

LEDA

That's astonishing. Why?

ALKMENA

I'm in love with my husband.

LEDA

Are you really? Oh, my dear—well, you can't go on being so exclusive forever so you might as well begin with a god.

ALKMENA

No, Leda. I'm unworthy of this honor. Now you are not only the most beautiful of reigning queens, you are also the most intelligent. Who but you could possibly work out a whole syntax, construct a grammar from a bird-call. You invented writing, didn't you?

LEDA

That's wasted on the gods because they haven't invented reading yet.

ALKMENA

You know astronomy. You know exactly where your zenith is and where your nadir. I'm always getting them mixed up. You have a scientific background. No, Leda, you're far more suitable for Jupiter than I am.

126

LEDA

I see—I'm beginning to understand— The more I see you, the more I listen to you, the more I begin to be persuaded that celestial contact might be fatal to your special charm. Yes, if you're still determined—I'll help you.

ALKMENA

Oh, Leda, Leda—

LEDA

On one condition.

ALKMENA

Condition?

LEDA

You must admit that I have the right to specify an incarnation that won't be repulsive to me.

ALKMENA

Oh, yes—

LEDA

In what form will Jupiter come?

ALKMENA

I don't know!

LEDA

You can know.

ALKMENA

How?

LEDA

He will assume some shape that haunts your desires and your dreams.

ALKMENA

But I'm not a haunted woman.

LEDA

Jupiter is so versatile. I hope it isn't a serpent. I have a horror of serpents. You can't count on me if it's a serpent! (*Rises.*)

ALKMENA

(*Rising*)

Leda, I have one weakness.

LEDA

What is it?

ALKMENA

My husband.

LEDA

Your husband? Your husband—what does he look like?

ALKMENA

My husband? What's he like? I haven't the faintest idea!

128

LEDA

Have you his portrait?

ALKMENA

Oh, yes—here. (*Shows medallion she is wearing on a chain around her neck.*)

LEDA

Is his hair blond?

ALKMENA

No, black like a raven's wing.

LEDA

He has those enigmatic eyes that I like.

ALKMENA

(*Taking medallion away rather quickly*)
He's not a god. He's my husband, Leda.

LEDA

Your husband, of course. Why didn't we think of that before? Your swan will be an Amphitryon. The first time your husband leaves home, Jupiter will enter your bedroom and you'll never know the difference.

ALKMENA

You terrify me. Amphitryon is away now!

LEDA

Away from Thebes?

ALKMENA

Yes, he left this morning for the war.

LEDA

When is he coming back?

ALKMENA

(*Looking over back wall*)

I haven't the faintest idea.

LEDA

You can't wage a war decently in less than two days!

ALKMENA

No, I'm afraid not.

LEDA

Before tonight I promise you that Jupiter will enter that door, so like Amphitryon that you will succumb to him.

ALKMENA

I couldn't possibly be deceived—I should know him.

LEDA

For once a human being will be a divine imitation, and you will be misled.

ALKMENA

Exactly. He'll be more perfect than Amphitryon, more noble than Amphitryon, and I shall hate him at first sight. (*Comes down to* LEDA.)

130

LEDA

And I tell you that with me he was a simply enormous swan and I couldn't distinguish him from the swan I see every day on my own river—

SOSIE

(Off stage)

News, Mistress, unexpected news! (*Entering.*)

ALKMENA

Amphitryon is here!

SOSIE

How did you know? I saw him leaping the moats on his galloping steed.

ALKMENA

No rider ever jumped them before!

SOSIE

One leap was enough for him.

LEDA

Is he alone?

SOSIE

Alone, but around him one could feel an invisible squadron. What shall I do?

ALKMENA

Go down the hill and meet him. (*Exit* SOSIE.)

131

LEDA

Now are you convinced? It's Jupiter, Jupiter the sham Amphitryon.

ALKMENA

Very well then he shall find here the sham Alkmena. Oh, Leda, I feel you are my friend. Don't friends do things like this for each other?

LEDA

Very often, but usually without saying a word about it! Your room's in there? (*She starts for bedroom.*)

ALKMENA

(*Following her*)

In there, in there.

LEDA

Are there steps going down? I have a horror of slipping in the dark.

ALKMENA

No, a smooth level floor. You mustn't weaken at the last moment, Leda.

LEDA

I have promised. I've never let a friend down yet! (*As she goes into bedroom*) This way—oh, yes, it's charming.

SOSIE

(*Off stage*)

Your horses, my lord, what shall I do with your horses? They're exhausted.

132

AMPHITRYON
(*Also off stage*)

Don't bother me about my horses, I shall be leaving again in a minute.

ALKMENA
(*Listening hard*)

He's lost interest in his horses, it's certainly not Amphitryon!

AMPHITRYON
(*Still off stage*)

Darling, it is I. (*He comes in. He goes to couch, throws down his cape and helmet.*)

ALKMENA

No one else. I can see that.

AMPHITRYON

Well, aren't you going to kiss me?

ALKMENA
(*Scrutinizing him, more and more amazed at the perfection of the imitation*)

Yes—in a minute. Let me look at you first. You're not afraid to show your face to your wife, are you? Your wife who is so familiar with it!

AMPHITRYON

Well—here it is.

133

ALKMENA

Yes—everything's there! Even those criss-crossed wrinkles, clawed by I know not what bird. Jupiter's eagle, I suppose.

AMPHITRYON

They're not eagle's feet, darling, they're crow's feet.

ALKMENA

Nevertheless, something's lacking—that scratch is lacking which he got yesterday. Strange husband that comes back from the war with one scratch less.

AMPHITRYON

(*Sits on couch and takes off his greaves*)
Nothing like fresh air for cuts.

ALKMENA

Marvellously healthy, isn't it, that outdoor exercise on a battlefield? What's going on behind that forehead—that forehead that is so much larger than usual?

AMPHITRYON

What always goes on—adoration for Alkmena.

ALKMENA

And what is that face thinking of—that face that gets bigger and bigger the more I look at it?

AMPHITRYON
(*Rises and goes to her*)

Of kissing your lips!

ALKMENA
(*Escaping from him*)

Why my lips?

AMPHITRYON
(*Follows more impetuously*)

Of biting the nape of your neck.

ALKMENA

Amphitryon, what's come over you? I've never heard you talk like this before.

AMPHITRYON

Alkmena, what's the matter?

ALKMENA

Where did you sleep last night?

AMPHITRYON

In the brambles—with a bundle of vine-shoots for a pillow. Oh, darling, I have to leave within the hour, for we're giving battle this morning. (*Close to her at last*) What is this sudden reserve between us? (*He seizes her and kisses her passionately*) You behave more like a fiancée than a wife.

ALKMENA
(*Horrified*)

What are you doing?

AMPHITRYON
(*Kisses her again*)
And now you're coming with me. (*Starts to take her to bedroom.*)

ALKMENA
(*Breaks away from him*)
Yes—one moment—I'll call you—my sweet—my lover—my husband. (*She exits, leaving* AMPHITRYON *alone. After a short pause* ALKMENA *calls to him from off stage*) Amphitryon!

AMPHITRYON
(*Eagerly*)
Yes, darling, here I am— (*He rushes after her. The stage is empty for a moment. Then* ALKMENA *re-enters from up stage. She comes down to below the couch.*)

ALKMENA
(*With great satisfaction*)
He is there—in her arms! Let me hear no more of the wickedness of life. Let me hear no more about fate—neither the wiles of men nor the caprices of the gods are proof against the clear love of a faithful wife. Echo, what have I to fear from men or gods if I'm faithful and loyal? Tell me, Echo, you who have never contradicted me. Nothing—isn't that so, Echo, nothing, nothing? (*Her arms are uplifted to the heavens.*)

ECHO
(*From off stage*)
Everything! Everything!

ALKMENA
(*Terrified*)

What? What is that you say?

ECHO
(*Relenting*)

Nothing! Nothing! (*Reassured,* ALKMENA *breathes a sigh of relief. Her arms are uplifted in gratitude, her face transfigured. The curtain falls.*)

ACT THREE

ACT THREE

Scene I

PLACE: *The roof of the Palace. A parapet, with one step up, runs around the roof. There are statues of heroes, gods and goddesses on the cornices of the roof. Their superb backs face the audience. A stone bench in the shape of an "H" stands in the center of the roof.*

TIME: *Later in the same day.*

NENETZA *and* KLEANTHA *are discovered looking down over the parapet. They are both laughing at something going on below, as* SOSIE *comes in.*

SOSIE

What are you doing here? Isn't there enough to do below? There are no flowers on Jupiter's altar and no garlands in the court-yard.

NENETZA

We came up to watch Queen Leda depart.

SOSIE

What if she stays all day?

KLEANTHA

There she goes; there she goes.

SOSIE

(*Getting between girls to look*)
She looks very self-satisfied, I must say.

KLEANTHA

Look at her, she's bowing to the lime trees!

NENETZA

No—the lime trees are bowing to her.

SOSIE

They're not bowing to her—they're bowing to the wind. Anybody'd think this was her day instead of our mistress'. (*Pushing them off*) Now, get down to your work. You, Nenetza, put amber in your mistress' bath and get out the big scarlet veil. (TRUMPETER *enters all out of breath. Stops, moistens his finger and holds it up.*)

TRUMPETER

Not a breath—not a breath of wind! On the roof, you'd think there'd be some air. (*He too peeps over the parapet*) In the streets, the festive banners are waving in the breeze and yet up here there's no breeze at all. It's strange.

SOSIE

Of course it's strange!

TRUMPETER

Do you hear the shouting?

142

SOSIE

Shouting? No!

TRUMPETER

Of course you can't, it's muffled by the clouds. Never have I seen the clouds so low. And yet, it's the greatest day that's ever come to Thebes. Our army is victorious—we have won a victory in one day. It's never been heard of before—and not a casualty. Even the horses have only been wounded in the left leg.

SOSIE

For once the recruiting slogans have come true. Great excitement in the streets!

TRUMPETER

Yes! Everything is arranged for Jupiter's arrival just as for an eclipse.

SOSIE

Do you think he will come in a burst of flame?

TRUMPETER

Probably. All the children are blackening bits of glass so that they'll be able to watch his arrival without it hurting their eyes.

SOSIE

I have mobilized all the unfortunates in Thebes—the halt, the lame and the blind. They are crowded around the Palace in the hope that Jupiter, in passing, will touch them and cure them. Even the paralytics I'm having carried up to the Palace.

TRUMPETER

Oh, but Sosie. I think that's a very bad idea!

SOSIE

Do you?

TRUMPETER

Yes. Jupiter thinks that man is perfect because he is created in his own image. If you reveal him now, in his imperfection, you may irritate him. You know how one detests a bad mirror. Do you know what I would do, Sosie, if I were you?

SOSIE

What?

TRUMPETER

(*Sits on bench beside* SOSIE)

Let it be announced that you are gathering the paralytics indeed and let these paralytics be a group of—lovely dancers! Then, don't you see, Sosie, Jupiter will not blush at having created a world so ridden with ugliness. He will have reason to be proud. He will think: "I've done pretty well."

SOSIE

There may be something in what you say, Trumpeter.

144

TRUMPETER

Oh, there is— What do you see now?

SOSIE

Alkmena is walking on the terrace.

TRUMPETER

What is her expression?

SOSIE

Expectant!

TRUMPETER
(*Blandly*)

Naturally!

SOSIE

And yet they say that she will refuse Jupiter.

TRUMPETER

That's coquetry—sheer coquetry!

SOSIE

They say she will refuse to conceive.

TRUMPETER

She can't refuse a thing like that!

SOSIE

Ah, but you don't know my mistress—she might. She's stubborn.

145

TRUMPETER

You don't know Jupiter. I know Jupiter. You don't know how stubborn he can be. That's what makes him a god! Stubborness! That's what distinguishes gods from men. If men could push obstinacy to the ultimate point they would be gods, too, like Jupiter. He'll stick to it. He'll have Alkmena's secret.

SOSIE
(Looking around him in awe)

Do you know, Trumpeter, I've been thinking—it sounds blasphemous to say it—but why do the gods come to Earth so often? Jupiter especially. Juno must be heavenly beautiful!

TRUMPETER
(Flatly)

Juno is his wife.

SOSIE

In that way the gods are like us. *(Confidentially)* Have you ever thought—if we had the privileges of the gods—if we were permitted to take different shapes and—you know what I mean, Trumpeter!

TRUMPETER

I follow you.

SOSIE

What shape would you take?

TRUMPETER

I think, Sosie, I'd be a butterfly! (ALKMENA *comes in. The* TRUMPETER *and* SOSIE *bow low to her.*)

TRUMPETER

Hail, mother-to-be!

SOSIE

Are there any further instructions, mistress?

ALKMENA

Instruction, Sosie?

SOSIE

For the arrival, mistress.

ALKMENA

What have you done so far, Sosie?

SOSIE

I am gathering together a group of the most exquisite dancers in all Thebes to greet Jupiter.

ALKMENA

How clever of you, Sosie.

TRUMPETER

(*Delighted, nudging* SOSIE)

What did I tell you, Sosie?

ALKMENA

Go, Sosie. Order the procession. And you, Trumpeter, help him, help him.

TRUMPETER

Delighted! It will be a garland day for Jupiter. (*They go out.* AMPHITRYON *enters. He is in very bad humor. He is scowling.*)

ALKMENA

Amphitryon, my darling! Why do you look like that. Aren't you going to kiss me?

AMPHITRYON

For the pleasure of kissing you I've paid heavily enough already.

ALKMENA

I've just ordered a processional in your honor. All the beauty in Thebes, my darling. Not many wives would do that. All Thebes is awaiting the arrival of the already departed god. I share a secret with Jupiter. Aren't you jealous that I share a secret with Jupiter?

AMPHITRYON

It's no secret that Jupiter is coming to you tonight. That's no secret. And you seem radiant at the prospect!

ALKMENA

I'm radiant at your return and I'm radiant over your victory.

AMPHITRYON

The victory was won in my absence. For this hour with you—

ALKMENA

This hour with me—?

AMPHITRYON

—cost me this victory. Had we been defeated in my absence, that I might have borne. But a victory without me—it's insupportable!

ALKMENA

But haven't you just come from the battlefield?

AMPHITRYON

What's the matter with you, Alkmena? Have you lost your senses? Have you forgotten already that I have just come from your arms?

ALKMENA

When did you return?

AMPHITRYON

You know perfectly well. You questioned me sufficiently about it. Are you so intoxicated by this honor that you don't remember these last few hours? I can't endure it!

ALKMENA

(*More to herself than to him*)
What have I done? What have I done?

AMPHITRYON

(*Turns, sees her distracted look. Misinterpreting its cause*)
Darling! I shall put up a fight with Jupiter, not physically—

mentally. I shall state my case. I have a voice, I have words—and for a general I'm highly articulate. I shall persuade Jupiter. I shall convince him!

ALKMENA

What I most fear is a conference between you and Jupiter. You've never persuaded anyone but me and you didn't do that by talking!

AMPHITRYON

Darling! Don't you realize that if we refuse—Jupiter might kill us.

ALKMENA

He can do worse than that!

AMPHITRYON

Worse?

ALKMENA

He could make us hate each other.

AMPHITRYON

He couldn't do that.

ALKMENA

He can. He can change us into beings that hate each other by instinct. A nightingale and a toad—a minnow and a shark—

AMPHITRYON

We would recognize each other—you and I.

ALKMENA

I, who eat with less enjoyment if you're using a spoon while I'm using a fork—what joy would there be left in life for me if you're breathing through gills and I through leaves— (*She begins to weep.*)

AMPHITRYON

Dearest, don't cry. If we submit to Jupiter—if we consent to this—he will leave us in peace—we shall be left with each other—we'd still have our love.

ALKMENA

No. How could we live with that between us? Imagine us with an unutterable third name always on our lips, withering our kisses, tarnished by immortality. How will you look at me when he who defiled us scrawls his signature across the sky in lightning? (*There is a clap of thunder.*)

AMPHITRYON

We've been so happy. I can't believe it's over!

ALKMENA

I should have loved us to have grown old together. To test the truth of the notion that people grow to look like each other, to experience the tranquil joys of nodding by the hearth, of dying finally. Oh, that wonderful old age of which Jupiter is about to rob us! Long, long years of marriage. Can you imagine us as two very old people? Tell me, my old husband, have you loved me?

AMPHITRYON

My whole life.

ALKMENA

Without exception?

AMPHITRYON

Without exception!

ALKMENA

Can I believe that?

AMPHITRYON

It's true.

ALKMENA

If it's true for you, then that shall be my truth also. Tell me, though, didn't you—just as we were about to celebrate our silver wedding—find a sixteen-year-old virgin, one of those girls at once bold and shy, who was ravished by your distinguished gray hair and your exploits in the past, a creature light as air and as enchanting as moonlight—a perfect monster, in fact?

AMPHITRYON

No, for me, you have always been younger than youth itself and I wanted us, when we reached old age, to have no reason for reproach between us.

152

ALKMENA

Nor have we— (*Kisses him*) not really. (*Another clap of thunder*) Now, at last, death may come; not surprising us, but catching up with us. Death may come!

ECHO

Death may come!

ALKMENA
(*Both rise*)

Echo tells us it is the end. And yet Echo deceived me once! (*There is a terrific crash of thunder.* AMPHITRYON *takes* ALKMENA *and walks down stage with her. Trumpets sound.* JUPITER *and* MERCURY *appear from behind the clouds and come down.*)

JUPITER
(*Looks at* AMPHITRYON)

Who is that possessive individual standing at her side?

MERCURY

It's her husband.

JUPITER

Amphitryon, the conqueror of the great battle of Corinth?

MERCURY

You're anticipating. He won't win Corinth—for five years yet. But it's he.

JUPITER

Who summoned him here?

MERCURY

Doubtless he came to offer you Alkmena personally.

AMPHITRYON

My Lord, Mercury is mistaken. I must defend Alkmena against you even if I die in the attempt.

JUPITER

Apparently you are not persuaded of the inevitability of this night.

AMPHITRYON

No, my Lord, I'm not!

MERCURY

(*To* JUPITER)

Jupiter, this is no moment for chatting. The sun is about to set.

JUPITER

The setting of the sun is my business.

MERCURY

But once the gods begin quibbling over ethics with mortals, the good old days are over.

JUPITER

My son is a stickler for etiquette. Quite right. (*To* AMPHITRYON) You know my power. You must realize that if I choose I can cause Alkmena to love me and even cause you to pray for my success as your rival. This conflict, therefore, between us is not one of matter but of form. It is not a question of whether I shall possess her—but how. Over such a slight technical formality for one little night, are you going to enter the lists with the gods?

AMPHITRYON

A general is not convinced by miracles!

JUPITER

Is that your last word? Do you really want to enter into a contest with me?

AMPHITRYON

If I have to—yes!

JUPITER

As a general, I think you are sufficiently intelligent not to risk battle with unequal forces. That's the A B C of tactics.

AMPHITRYON

I prefer that other technical formality—death!

JUPITER

You must understand my forbearance. I'm fond of you both. As a couple, I'm rather proud of you. I am pleased with the idea of your two superbly sculptured bodies, like prows on galleons, cleaving great furrows in time. I want to sponsor you. It is as a good friend that I wish to be established with you both.

AMPHITRYON

You are already so established and revered. I refuse!

JUPITER

You deny to Alkmena the privileges accident has thrown in your way, when you yourself are not so blameless.

ALKMENA

(*Fearing* JUPITER's *revelation of her trick with* LEDA *she breaks away from* AMPHITRYON *and approaches* JUPITER)
Jupiter!

JUPITER

Very well, Mercury, let the truth be blazoned forth to all the world—last night's truth and today's— (MERCURY *is about to comply when* ALKMENA *makes a last effort to stop him.*)

ALKMENA

(*Drops to her knees before* JUPITER)
Jupiter—can we be alone?

JUPITER

We shall be. (*He waves his hand.* MERCURY *and* AMPHITRYON *disappear.* JUPITER *offers* ALKMENA *his hand. She takes it and then sits with him on bench.*)

JUPITER

Alone at last!

ALKMENA

If one is to believe the legends—it is a kind of solitude which you experience often. Oh, Jupiter, with so many, why do you choose me for an historic role to which I am so little suited?

JUPITER

Because you endow the historic with an air of impromptu which absolutely delights me!

ALKMENA

Why destroy a perfect marriage—leave it in ruins—for one moment's pleasure?

JUPITER

Isn't that the essence of all love?

ALKMENA

Suppose I offer you more than love—better than love—

JUPITER

Am I so repulsive to you?

ALKMENA

If you only were.

JUPITER

You would resist me then because you love me?

ALKMENA

Love! Love you may experience with anyone. But between us I would like to create a bond that is sweeter and more powerful; I, alone among women, can offer you this—I do offer it—and it's friendship!

JUPITER

Friendship? I hear it for the first time. Explain it. What does it mean? Is it a word current on Earth?

ALKMENA

The expression is current.

JUPITER

What is its object?

ALKMENA

To bring together the most totally dissimilar people and make them equal. Have you never seen the most ill-assorted creatures isolate themselves for no reason at all? A cabinet minister and a gardener—a lion sharing his cage with a poodle? And these misfits have a perfect community of interests—they seem drawn together by some strange, chemical substance in their bodies.

JUPITER

I vaguely remember a cabinet minister and a gardener, yes, they were diverting to watch.

ALKMENA

They'd stroll down the hundred paces of the garden path and then—stroll back again.

JUPITER

The cabinet minister would converse learnedly about pruning and weeds—

ALKMENA

—the gardener of filibusters and excise taxes—

JUPITER

—then after each had had his say, they'd finally stop at the end of the path—

ALKMENA

—look affectionately into each other's eyes—

JUPITER

—stroke their beards—

ALKMENA

—and wink.

JUPITER

Friendship?

ALKMENA

Friendship!

JUPITER

It sounds an amusing novelty. But if I became your friend—what would we do?

ALKMENA

First of all, instead of believing in you as a god, I should think of you as a friend. My thoughts of you would be from the heart, whereas my prayers to you would no longer be repeated by rote but addressed to you—personally. Instead of ritual gestures of obeisance I should—beckon you with my hands.

JUPITER

Are you sure that wouldn't take up too much of your time?

ALKMENA

Oh, no. I'd find the time.

JUPITER

And I? What would I do?

ALKMENA

Well . . . on days when I didn't feel like seeing anybody at all—then you'd come—you'd sit at the foot of my divan, calmly.

JUPITER

Would we just sit?

ALKMENA

No, we'd talk.

JUPITER

What about?

ALKMENA

Well, you'd tell me your joys, your sorrows and your burdens. You would explain Creation to me.

160

JUPITER

You are interested in Creation?

ALKMENA

Oh, yes. (*He smiles*) Why do you smile?

JUPITER

Nothing. And then?

ALKMENA

Then you would go away. *But you would have been there.*
Do you understand?

JUPITER
(*Laughs*)

Faintly.

ALKMENA

I see you're still a little vague about it.

JUPITER

I'm afraid so—

ALKMENA

Well, suppose I give you some examples of how I'd call on
you for help and you tell me what you'd do.

JUPITER

Perhaps that would be better.

ALKMENA

(ALKMENA *clasps her hands in front of her*)
Are you ready?

JUPITER

(*Sees her clasped hands and does the same with his*)
Yes, I am ready.

ALKMENA

My husband is lost. What can you do for me?

JUPITER

As a friend?

ALKMENA

As a friend.

JUPITER

I would dispatch a comet to guide him. I would endow you with second sight so you could see him. I would increase the volume of your voice so that no matter where he was, you could talk to him.

ALKMENA

Is that all you'd do?

JUPITER

I'd bring him back!

ALKMENA

That's better— Now—a child of mine is ill?

JUPITER

I'd drape the universe in sadness. Flowers would lose their scent. The very animals, dejected, would drag their heads.

ALKMENA

You wouldn't go so far as to cure the child?

JUPITER

Of course I would. How stupid of me!

ALKMENA

Oh, no, no. You're not stupid. In the main, you've done very well.

JUPITER

Thank you.

ALKMENA

One more question!

JUPITER

Yes?

ALKMENA

In a marriage ideally happy, a husband has been unfaithful through no fault of his own—what can you do for him?

JUPITER

Cause him never to know it.

ALKMENA

Ah, Jupiter, you are a friend—a true friend!

JUPITER

It seems to me, I'd have more to do than you would.

ALKMENA

Naturally, since you have more power. To do more than one's share is one of the privileges of friendship. Have you never tasted the strange joy of submitting to the will of another?

JUPITER

I've never had the opportunity.

ALKMENA

You have it now. Shall you miss it?

JUPITER

I see through you, Alkmena, I read your thoughts.

ALKMENA

You see, you know my secrets. Therefore you are so much more suited to be my friend than my lover.

JUPITER

I see that no matter what I do, I cannot cross the immutable line that separates us. Therefore, I free you.

164

ALKMENA

(*Overjoyed, rises*)

Oh! (*Drops to her knees before him.*)

JUPITER

You've touched me, somehow. You are stubborn, you are obstinate. But you also are forlorn in your devotion. You make fidelity affecting. If you can console the Thebans for depriving them so brutally of this national honor—I give you my word. . . . (*Rises*) I shall not impose my presence on you tonight.

ALKMENA

(*Rises also*)

But why need the Thebans know? Let me appear before them—before the whole world as your mistress. True, it will drive them wild with jealousy, and you know how trying envy can be; but, on the other hand, it'll give Amphitryon and me great pleasure to suffer this inconvenience for you. That's friendship!

JUPITER

You dazzle me, Alkmena. How you fleck your little tricks with gleams of loyalty. How you flavor your little lies with a tincture of sincerity! Nevertheless, I free you!

ALKMENA

Without reservations?

JUPITER

Without reservations.

ALKMENA
(Suspicious)
But you accept so easily—without a struggle.

JUPITER
It is your special gift, Alkmena, to teach even the gods resignation.

ALKMENA
Yes, but you're eager—you're more than resigned—you're eager—

JUPITER
You make friendship sound so attractive, it satisfies me.

ALKMENA
You seem so easily satisfied at the prospect of not being my lover.

JUPITER
No, it's not that—it's only that—you are so determined.

ALKMENA
Jupiter—?

JUPITER
Yes, Alkmena.

ALKMENA
Are you sure that you've never been my lover?

166

JUPITER

Why do you ask me that?

ALKMENA

Because my knowledge of men leads me to believe that when they're as noble as this, it's because they're already satisfied.

JUPITER

Already?

ALKMENA

Are you sure that you have never taken the shape of Amphitryon?

JUPITER

Quite sure.

ALKMENA

You have so many affairs—maybe you did, and it slipped your mind.

JUPITER

(*Admonishingly*)

Alkmena!

ALKMENA

Because I must admit that if I felt you had not, I should feel a certain regret.

JUPITER

Regret?

ALKMENA

Yes. To have been loved by the Master of the Gods himself
—through no fault of my own—would be quite a feather in
the cap of a middle-class housewife! (*Laughs*) It's too bad!

JUPITER

You are only trying to trap me.

ALKMENA

(*Rises, quick as a flash*)
You are capable, then, of being caught?

JUPITER

I have never been—your lover!

ALKMENA

Jupiter—take me in your arms.

JUPITER

(*Obeying*)
Are you at home there?

ALKMENA

Yes.

JUPITER

Yes?—only yes?

ALKMENA

Yes, Jupiter, darling—there you see—it seems quite natural,
for me to be calling you darling.

168

JUPITER

Quite natural.

ALKMENA

It sprang from me spontaneously. What is this pleasurable sensation that flows through my body when I'm near you? Whence does it come?

JUPITER

We are sympatico.

ALKMENA

What's that?

JUPITER

A friendly word in a language that does not yet exist. It means that we understand each other very well.

ALKMENA

Why, then, in spite of this harmony, am I so troubled?

JUPITER

Perhaps because I am beginning to take the form of Amphitryon. Perhaps because you're beginning to fall in love with me.

ALKMENA

No, it's not the beginning of something—it's the end of something. Confess, Jupiter, wasn't it you yourself that came to me after the great fire in Thebes?

JUPITER

No. Neither was it I who rescued the little boy from the sea.

ALKMENA

You see, you know about it!

JUPITER

(*Toying with a lock of her hair*)

Don't I know everything that concerns you? Alas, no—it was your husband. How soft your hair is!

ALKMENA

It seems to me—I have a conviction—it's not the first time you've twisted that lock of hair or leaned over me like this. Was it at night or was it at dawn you came?

JUPITER

Neither! Neither!

ALKMENA

You have obscured everything for me. My whole body rejoices at having met you. I am thrilled in my being at this hour—and yet I'm conscious also of trouble, of uncertainty—of something. . . . Can you not rid my mind of this uncertainty?

JUPITER

Since you will not believe me, I can grant you forgetfulness.

ALKMENA

Yes, that's what I want most of all, Jupiter—forgetfulness!

170

JUPITER

I shall obliterate your past—shall I also reveal to you your future?

ALKMENA

No! No!

JUPITER

It will be a happy one, believe me.

ALKMENA

I know what a happy future consists of. My beloved husband will live and die. My dear son will be born and live and die. I shall live and die.

JUPITER

Since I cannot share your mortal life with you, will you not, for an instant, share the life of the gods? Since your whole past is about to sink into oblivion, do you not wish to see in one flash of clarity the whole world—past, present and future—and to comprehend its meaning?

ALKMENA

No, I'm not curious.

JUPITER

Do you not wish to see humanity at its labors, from its birth to its final dissolution? Do you not wish to see the eleven great beings who will constitute the finest ornament in all history? One with his lovely Jewish face; another with her little nose from Lorraine?

ALKMENA
(Sighs)

No!

JUPITER

And since you are about to forget everything, do you not wish to understand the illusions that constitute your virtue and your happiness?

ALKMENA

No—no—

JUPITER

Nor at this last moment what I really am to you?

ALKMENA

No—forgetfulness, Jupiter; I beg of you—forgetfulness—

JUPITER

And I beg you, Alkmena, do not abandon me; do not leave me with nothing on my hands but my divinity.

ALKMENA

I must—as you must abandon me to my humanity.

JUPITER

I will kiss you. Only this way can I grant forgetfulness. It is the conventional ritual. Forget everything you have lived—everything you wish forgotten. *(Kisses her)* Except this kiss!

172

ALKMENA

What kiss?

JUPITER

You know perfectly well. That kiss I took the trouble to put this side of oblivion. (JUPITER *lifts his arm in an Olympian gesture. Music is heard.* MERCURY *and* AMPHITRYON *appear—each from opposite sides of the stage.* JUPITER, ALKMENA *by his side, addresses* AMPHITRYON) She has won me over, Amphitryon, and I rejoice in my defeat. Is she always like this?

AMPHITRYON

She generally manages to be right!

MERCURY

The whole of Thebes is at the foot of the Palace clamoring for you to appear with Alkmena in your arms.

JUPITER

My son and his ceremonials!

MERCURY

Just show yourselves—that will satisfy them completely.

JUPITER
(*To* AMPHITRYON)

Do you mind?

AMPHITRYON

It is an honor.

JUPITER

Thank you, General! (*He offers his arm to* ALKMENA; *they walk to parapet to display themselves to the populace*) Bear up, Alkmena, for this one instant only.

ALKMENA

These wretches that insult my integrity!

JUPITER

Even they demand their legend.

MERCURY

Just say a few words to them; you can be brief, you know—they'll elaborate it themselves. (*Prompting*) At last I meet you—

JUPITER AND MERCURY
(*Together*)

At last I meet you, dearest Alkmena . . .

MERCURY

Yes, dear Jupiter . . .

ALKMENA AND MERCURY

Yes, dear Jupiter, and so we have to part.

MERCURY
(*Prompting*)

And so begins this night—

MERCURY AND JUPITER

So begins this night—so fertile for all the world.

MERCURY AND ALKMENA

So ends this day—this day that I was beginning to love.

MERCURY

Kiss! (JUPITER *kisses* ALKMENA *on the forehead.*)

JUPITER

(*Leading her back to* AMPHITRYON)

And now that the legend has been duly established, befitting the dignity of the gods—

MERCURY

Amphitryon, your marriage—blessed already—is to be blessed even further—

JUPITER

Alkmena is to bear you a son. Will you name him to please me? Will you name him Hercules?

AMPHITRYON

Hercules?

ALKMENA

Hercules!

JUPITER

And I shall be his . . . godfather . . .

175

JUPITER AND MERCURY
(*Together*)
... and so will destiny be fulfilled! (AMPHITRYON *and*
ALKMENA *are in each other's arms.* JUPITER, *followed by* MER-
CURY, *goes to back toward the low-hanging clouds.*)

JUPITER
We must intrude no longer on these two—I have withheld
their night too long already— (*The lights slowly dim.* JUPITER
commands the firmament) Curtain of the night descend—
but for an instant let them be encircled in a glade of light!
(*Light from above falls on* AMPHITRYON *and* ALKMENA) A
little island of fidelity! My arm embraces them to bring them
closer to their joy—this untarnished couple—forever to remain untarnished! (JUPITER *and* MERCURY *are now on their
way to the Empyrean.*)

MERCURY
But I warn you—posterity will gossip!

JUPITER
Alkmena won't mind. By that time she will have forgotten
even my farewell. (*He disappears aloft, followed by* MERCURY,
trailing celestial rays.)

ALKMENA
(*Transfigured for the moment by the divine, flings up her
arms and calls after the departed god*)
Farewell, Jupiter, farewell!

Curtain